The Arts in Education

Do the arts improve academic achievement? What does it mean to 'teach' art? What should be the balance of classical and pop be in the music curriculum? Should we encourage young children on the stage? How do we judge whether what a child produces is good? How do we justify the arts in the curriculum? What should be the balance between form and content when teaching art?

The arts in education inspire considerable commitment and passion. However, this is not always matched by clarity of understanding. In this book Mike Fleming introduces the reader to key theoretical questions associated with arts education and clearly explains how these are related to practice. It offers an authoritative account of how ideas relevant to education are addressed by key authors in aesthetics, art theory and cultural studies.

Covering all aspects of arts education, the book considers:

- definitions and theories of art;
- influences on teaching the arts;
- researching the arts;
- teaching and learning;
- creativity;
- assessment.

Throughout the book there are examples of practice to illustrate key ideas and a discussion of useful background texts with a summary of content and arguments for further exploration. Written by a leading authority in the field, it is essential reading for students on Arts PGCE and M Level courses, teachers of the arts and policy developers that require more understanding and insight into their practice.

Mike Fleming is Emeritus Professor in the School of Education at the University of Durham, UK.

The Arts in Education

An introduction to aesthetics, theory and pedagogy

Mike Fleming

Routledge
Taylor & Francis Group
LONDON AND NEW YORK

First published 2012
by Routledge
2 Park Square, Milton Park, Abingdon, Oxon OX14 4RN

Simultaneously published in the USA and Canada
by Routledge
711 Third Avenue, New York, NY 10017

Routledge is an imprint of the Taylor & Francis Group, an informa business

British Library Cataloguing in Publication Data
A catalogue record for this book is available from the British Library

Library of Congress Cataloging in Publication Data
Fleming, Michael (Michael P.)
An introduction to the arts in education: aesthetics, theory and pedagogy / Mike Fleming.
p. cm.
Includes bibliographical references and index.
1. Arts in education. 2. Arts—Study and teaching (Elementary) 3. Arts—Study and teaching (Secondary) I. Title.
NX280.F59 2012
700.71—dc23
2011036166

ISBN 978-0-415-62028-4 (hbk)
ISBN 978-0-415-62029-1 (pbk)
ISBN 978-0-203-12624-0 (ebk)

Typeset in Bembo
by Book Now, London

MIX
Paper from
responsible sources
FSC   FSC® C004839
www.fsc.org

Printed and bound in Great Britain by
TJ International Ltd, Padstow, Cornwall

To Marianne

Contents

Tables

Acknowledgements

I am grateful to many cohorts of MA and doctoral students at the School of Education, Durham University for their enthusiasm and feedback. My wife Marianne made valuable suggestions to improve the text. I owe thanks to David Parker, Julian Sefton-Green and other staff at Creative Partnerships whose commission in 2008 was a considerable source of motivation. I am also grateful to the editor of *Journal of Aesthetic Education* whose support in 2006 was also encouraging. I owe a debt to a large number of authors, which I hope is adequately acknowledged in the book itself. I have found writings by Lyas, McGilchrist and Shusterman particularly inspiring; their work has much relevance for education. I have been fortunate in having a long association with David Fulton / Routledge and I am grateful to Annamarie Kino and her team for excellent support and encouragement.

Introduction

The arts have a strong claim to be part of education. They enrich our understanding of the world, challenge prevailing ideologies, widen our perspectives, engage and delight us, and celebrate our humanity. Such claims are valid but in themselves do not add much to our understanding of art and its proper place in education. They may induce enthusiastic assent from people who connect with them but to others they may sound like empty rhetoric. They also leave many questions unanswered. Does all art function in this way? Or is it just specific forms or works of a particular quality? Does art have a unique claim to these aspirations? For example, does not science also enrich our understanding of the world? Once we consider the more focused implications of seeing art as part of education, a series of other questions come to mind. What should count as 'art' in school? How do we judge whether what a child produces is good? Should we make such judgements? Are some art forms more important than others? Do the arts improve academic achievement? What does it mean to *teach* art? The central aim of this book is to contribute to our understanding of the arts in education by addressing these and a host of other questions.

It is tempting to rush into discussion of these questions but first some consideration of what is meant both by 'understanding' and by 'the arts in education' will be helpful. Words and phrases of this kind can lead us into making unwarranted assumptions. The fact that when we use the word 'understanding', people generally understand what we say seems to suggest that the word has one fixed, core meaning. That is far from being the case. When we say we understand a problem, a painting, a set of travel directions, a foreign language or a friend, the sense is slightly different in each case. Within this variety there are two broad uses of the term that are particularly illuminating when thinking about arts and education. There is one sense of 'understanding' that means 'coming to see clearly' as when we speak about 'getting' a joke or a problem. However, when I say of someone 'I am starting to understand you' I may mean rather the opposite, not that I have exhausted what there is to know about you but that I am starting to see a more complex person than I had first thought. In this latter sense understanding is not an event and certainly not an 'all or nothing' affair but more akin to an extended process. When we see understanding not as a form of colonisation of knowledge but more as a process of refining and deepening, of seeing things from new angles and making fresh connections there are important implications for education in general and more specifically for pedagogy.

The narrower use of 'understanding' is more likely to involve analysing, taking things apart, providing an exhaustive explanation. The other has more to do with a holistic vision, making links with our own experience, seeing how things fit together. The first has to do with 'getting to the bottom of', whereas the other inclines more towards seeing greater depth. There are also different processes involved: one depends on logical elucidation and clarity of explanation, the other relies more on demonstrating and showing connections through examples. The two uses of 'understanding' (which can be called 'analytic' and 'synthetic' in short) are not mutually exclusive but the distinction is not trivial. If we approach an art work with the expectation of understanding it in the sense of acquiring a full and complete logical explanation we will often be either bewildered or disappointed. Moreover, if we see 'understanding' simply as an event that culminates in clear and unambiguous outcomes, our teaching may become narrow, expository and mechanical.

Notwithstanding the limitations of seeing 'understanding' only in a narrow way, the two processes are both important. This book is written in discursive language so it does seek to probe and explain issues clearly and rationally. However, it also recognises the importance of the more holistic vision that relies on showing as much as saying and that aims at expanding perspectives and posing questions rather than just forming easy conclusions. An underlying argument of this book is that both perspectives and processes are needed. This can be seen clearly in relation to pedagogy. Some teachers of the arts are good at engaging students in exciting activities but less successful at ensuring focused learning, understanding and progression. On the other hand, an approach which attends to detail without a sense of a bigger picture or animated purpose may leave students bored and uninspired.

As well as 'understanding', the concept of 'arts in education' needs some explicit discussion because there is no obvious consensus on what should count as 'art' in this context. Dance, drama, visual art and music are the usual contenders, but where does this leave literature, which invariably is seen as art but is more often found within the language curriculum? In the UK, dance has traditionally been placed within the physical education rather than the arts curriculum; does designating an activity as 'art' change the way we see it and teach it? What of contemporary media such as television and film, and forms of expression based on new technologies? What about architecture, sculpture and photography or, more controversially, graffiti and body art? Should the arts curriculum reflect the full range of arts in contemporary society or do schools have a duty to teach what is considered the best? There are clearly theoretical issues related to definitions of art, the relationship between high and popular art, and judgement of quality that need to be addressed.

As well as the issue of what to include in the category of 'arts', there is a prior question of whether it makes sense at all to group the arts together in this way. It may be argued that it is at the individual art subject level that the really important questions related to justification and teaching occur. After all there have been far more books on the teaching of the individual arts in the last 20 years than on the arts in education as a whole. One of the enemies to understanding is a tendency to over-generalise, making the assumption that what can be said about teaching one art subject applies equally to all of them. A moment's reflection tells us that what may be true of one art form related to one specific age group may not necessarily be true of all the arts. Similarly, what may be true of art in one cultural context may not be true elsewhere. On the other hand, our ability to generalise in some form is the starting point for any understanding, otherwise we would be able to say nothing of a broad, theoretical nature. It is enough at this stage to say that the question of whether we are justified in using a generic category of the 'arts in education' will not be taken for granted and will be a theme addressed at various points in this book.

It is not just the term 'arts in education' that some may argue is redundant but also the term 'art' itself. The idea of 'art' and the 'aesthetic' is associated in some people's minds with high art, elitism and bourgeois values. If we accept that the concept of 'art' is not confined to the classical canon of Beethoven, Shakespeare and Rembrandt we are faced with the question of whether it is possible at all to draw boundaries. What justification is there for excluding within the definition of art such contenders as soap operas, romantic novels, action films, comedy shows, comics and adverts? Is it all not just 'culture' and would not the word 'culture' be more appropriate for the twenty-first century than 'arts'? On the face of it, teachers seem to be confronting an impossible choice between subscribing to elitism on the one hand and embracing relativism on the other. One of the arguments pursued in this book is that the spectre of relativism embraced by so much modern theory of the last 40 years casts a pernicious influence on the teaching of the arts. However, the discussion will also suggest that old-fashioned elitism is not the only alternative.

This book stays with convention in being divided into different chapters that appear to follow a linear sequence. However, these chapters are not intended to be discrete, nor was it possible to find a sequence that proved to be just right. The chapters are organically linked with a number of themes interwoven. It will be helpful to identify three of the main themes that reappear at different points in the book. The first of these has to do with the nature of language and meaning. As the discussion of 'understanding' and 'arts in education' illustrated, the mere existence of a word does not mean that it has one fixed, static meaning. Meaning is determined in use and words and related concepts shift in meaning in different contexts. This has consequences for the way we approach discussion of art. For though it may be tempting to assume that we can get better clarity by pinning things down with narrow definitions, this often serves to restrict our vision. It is often more helpful to ask not 'what is art? what is creativity? what is expression?' but instead to ask 'what are the consequences, particularly for teaching, of seeing art, creativity, expression in this or that way?' This view of language also contributes to the tone of the book, which aims to be exploratory and probing rather than argumentative or confrontational. The primary reason is not for the sake of courtesy, important though that is, but emanates more from the underlying view of language. Many statements about art, as will be revealed in subsequent chapters, turn out to be both true and not true, informative in some senses but misleading in others.

A second cross-chapter theme is the distinction between what might be termed 'analytic' and 'synthetic' approaches identified earlier in the discussion of understanding. This distinction can be usefully applied to responding to art, teaching the arts and theoretical discussion of art. There is a popular view still surviving from accounts of art that originated in the eighteenth century that response to art should be somehow 'pure' – in other words we must respond to the work as if we are doing a practical criticism in school, without being contaminated by historical and contextual detail and by what critics have to say. This view is in one sense daft. However, it also contains an element of truth in that it seems to point to the need for some sort of genuine, authentic response that is deeply felt and not imported from outside. This distinction also carries over to the responsibilities we have as teachers of art in helping students to make genuine, holistic, synthetic, heartfelt responses but also recognising the need for judicious intervention, judging how and when it is right to insist on close, informed analysis. Such judgements are not determined by simple rules but require sensitivity to specific contexts.

Finally, the analytic/synthetic distinction can be applied to theoretical discussion of art. We do need to try to examine issues systematically and with clarity. However, that needs to happen with a degree of humility and with a sense of the provisional nature of knowledge. We need to recognise, as Wittgenstein did in relation to philosophy, that theory can get in the way of understanding, and send us completely in the wrong direction. A lot of artists and lovers of art do not seem to need a detailed grasp of theory for a rich and fulfilling life in art. That much is true but I do believe that our thinking can be expanded, prejudices challenged and fulfilment enriched if theory is approached in the right way. There is also a special responsibility on teachers of the arts to try to understand what they are doing and why they are doing it.

A third theme that underlies all the chapters is a concern with the relationship between theory and practice. This is not a book about practice in the sense that it is a detailed discussion of how to teach the arts; there are excellent books on the market that do that very well. However, it is a book about practice in that the theoretical discussion is driven by a pragmatic concern to explore the implications of theoretical positions for pedagogy. There are some outstanding classical and contemporary art theorists who do not write directly about education but whose work has a huge amount to say that is useful for teachers. One of the aims of this book is to make some of those connections, with the hope that readers who do not know their work will be motivated to seek it out.

The chapter headings are fairly wide-ranging but, even so, there were other contenders for inclusion. I did consider whether there ought to be a separate chapter on the influence of technology on arts practice but opted instead for integrating this issue because it has implications for various topics such as the changing nature of how we conceptualise art, on the high-art / low-art debate and on the general theme of pluralism. The aims of the book are both modest and challenging in equal measure. It attempts to say a lot about a variety of topics but it does not attempt to have the last word or to be comprehensive in its coverage. As befits an introductory text, it aims to point readers in fruitful directions for further enquiry.

I have used the terms 'teaching' and 'teachers' several times in this introduction. However, the intended audience for the book is not confined specifically to classroom teachers. One of the encouraging developments in arts education in recent years is the increased emphasis on partnership between artists, artistic companies and schools. However, the arguments about the need for understanding apply equally to all participants. The intention is that this book will have something useful to say to arts teachers, lecturers, policy developers, community workers and artists who require more understanding and insight into their practice.

Although most of the examples are UK based, the focus is not intended to be too restricted or local. There are very interesting national developments in arts education happening in Australia at the present time. Some of the most passionate advocacy for the arts in education comes from the USA. In Singapore considerable resources are being allocated to the development of the arts. Many countries in Europe are undergoing curriculum reform and are considering the place of the arts in education. A perspective from non-western countries on the arts and creativity is very illuminating. What is common to many countries is that the arts are not always taken as seriously as they should be. They largely do not provoke outright hostility – as Eisner (2002: xi) said no one wants to be regarded as philistine – but a rather damaging bland assent. It is hoped that the book will have something valuable to say in a variety of education contexts, including why the arts in education are generally undervalued. The book is more concerned with general theoretical questions than concrete issues of funding, organisation and policy development, although the further reading sections will have recommendations in those areas.

The further reading sections are intended to be precisely that – reading beyond the texts that are discussed in the body of the chapters. In other words, I have not chosen to include references to books and papers simply to expose their weaknesses. Life is too short; paper is too valuable. All of the texts that are referenced have something useful to tell us about art theory and practice and are worth reading.

Chapter 1 focuses on justifying the arts. The questions 'why should we teach the arts?' or 'why should we teach this particular art form?' seem simple enough on the surface. They are questions that advocates of the arts are often asked to consider and address. One response is to present a list of reasons, but such a list can easily become long and overambitious. Furthermore, a long list of reasons may hide important questions that should be considered. The chapter will consider different polarities that have arisen when the issue of justification has been considered. Should we place more emphasis on 'feeling' or 'cognition', on 'making' or 'responding', on 'intrinsic' or 'extrinsic' arguments? Does the concept of the 'aesthetic' have too many traditional, ideological resonances to be useful in the context of education?

Chapter 2 examines previous attempts to define art precisely and how these have given way to a much better grasp of the fluid nature of the concept. But what are the implications of this view for teaching art in schools? The chapter discusses concepts of representation, form, expression and institutional theories of art. Whereas each of these theories does not offer a complete explanation of what 'art' means, they all provide valuable insights into issues related to the teaching of the arts. This chapter will also explore implications for education of 'separatist' (a view that sees art as something more rarefied and special) and 'inclusive' (a view that is more grounded and links art with life and with its social context more closely) accounts.

Chapter 3 turns to an examination of the theoretical influences on the teaching of the arts. It considers the primary influence of progressive thinking and the legacy that was left, with a tendency to emphasise creating or self-expression rather than responding to art produced by others. The progressive influence diminished the role of the teacher. The chapter considers what it means to teach art and how students should be taught to participate in the cultural world in which they will live, with its diverse range of forms and types of art. The chapter situates this discussion within a consideration of contemporary cultural theory and issues of high and low art.

Chapter 4 considers different conceptions of research and the use made of the arts in the research process itself before discussing some of the empirical research on the arts in education. Classic distinctions between science and art, the analytic and synthetic can help elucidate different opinions about what counts as research and provide further insight into ways of conceptualising knowledge and meaning. This chapter therefore, despite its title, does not sit outside the main issues addressed elsewhere in the book. Themes that have emerged as important in the discussion of the arts, such as the general and particular, the nature of understanding and the importance of context, are central to a consideration of the place of research.

Chapter 5 examines ways in which an historical perspective may help illuminate understanding of arts in education. An exploration of the history of art itself and history of ideas about art are closely related but can help highlight changing ways in which art and the artist were seen at different times. The brief history of arts in education focuses specifically on the UK on the grounds that such a discussion has to take place in a specific context. Even so, there are dangers of over-generalising, but some consideration of past tensions can illuminate current theory and practice.

Chapter 6 addresses an issue explicitly that has emerged in previous chapters related to conceptions of *learning in* and *learning through* the arts. This will provide a focus for more detailed discussion of inclusive/separatist conceptions of art in schools; extrinsic/ intrinsic justification; and creating and responding. The concepts of learning in and learning through provide useful theoretical perspectives on the teaching of the arts as well as useful tools for evaluating practice. Although the two constructs overlap to some degree, they provide an indication of potential pitfalls when the elements associated with one approach dominate at the expense of the other.

Chapter 7 focuses on the thorny concept of creativity. As well as addressing problems of definition it explores how the concept can be either useful or useless in education. Uses of the term 'creativity' may inadvertently affect practice by either limiting possibilities or extending them too far. The first section of the chapter focuses on the wider context of education where the concept of creativity is being increasingly applied, before focusing more specifically on arts education. The chapter does not form a comprehensive review of the literature but rather aims to highlight the more relevant debates.

Chapter 8 addresses the equally thorny issue of assessment. The arts in education have to function within education in a contemporary culture of assessment with an emphasis on clear learning outcomes, targets and testing. Assessment often causes tension and disagreement because of the diverse and demanding functions that it is expected to fulfil. These differences can be compounded in the context of art because the aims and range of outcomes are particularly complex. The issues facing teachers of the arts with regard to assessment can be informed by writing on the arts that has addressed issues related to subjectivity and objectivity and making judgements.

Chapter 9 will examine different art subjects individually with a view to establishing their distinct value. It will give some consideration to ways in which arts are categorised in education and argument about whether the arts should be seen as a generic group. Traditionally, the subjects identified as 'arts' in an education context in official policy documents are dance, drama, music and visual arts. However, this leaves 'literature' in an ambiguous position and may exclude hybrid forms.

Chapter 10 returns to the distinction between analytic and synthetic approaches to understanding addressed in the Introduction and relates these to a wider perspective. It summarises the key tensions and differences of emphasis which have been discussed in previous chapters and the implications for practice. It also relates changing conceptions of art to pluralism and links the ethical role of art in society to an intercultural perspective.

1

Justifying the arts

Introduction

Recently a colleague of mine told me about a lesson she observed in a secondary school. The teacher was in the middle of directing the class of 13-year-olds through a series of art-related activities when one of the students interrupted the proceedings. He asked the teacher to provide an 'intellectual justification' for the activity declaring that what he was being required to do was 'babyish'. The teacher sent him out of the room.

To fully understand what was going on here would need more details of the lesson and tasks, the precise context and the attitude of the pupil. Confidentiality forbids such details but the incident, even as it stands, raises interesting issues. It is easy to be shocked by the teacher's response but we need to acknowledge that a flawed human reaction will sometimes take the place of a textbook response: the head does not always rule the heart. It is not uncommon for pupils to ask rather half-heartedly 'why do we have to do this?' but the request for an 'intellectual justification' puts this response into a different league. Perhaps the pupil had a point and the teacher was floundering incoherently much like the drama teacher in *Summer Heights High* in Chris Lilley's wicked satire (available on YouTube). Alternatively this may be a pupil unduly influenced by a system obsessed with outcomes and narrow utility, failing to relax and enjoy himself and failing to understand that asking for a justification of isolated activities in this way is simply misguided. Or perhaps he was just being obstreperous.

Those of us who work in the arts can feel a little vulnerable or tongue-tied when asked for justification of a particular lesson or project. More often than not the reason is not a lack of understanding but precisely the opposite, an intuitive sense of the density of the issue. A discursive explanation can seem either prosaic or overblown and certainly will never be enough to convince a sceptic; it may be tempting to take the view 'you either get it or you don't'. However, ignoring issues of justification is politically naïve and dangerous from the point of view of pedagogy because unless one examines in an explicit way questions related to overall purpose it is all too easy for teaching to be directed by implicit views in unhelpful ways. A music or literature curriculum that is dominated by the classical canon may be driven by unexamined notions of high art. Or a drama syllabus that is focused exclusively on creating drama instead of including responding to the work of others may be unwittingly motivated by limited theories of expression. In the lesson described at the start of this chapter, the teacher may have had nothing more to underpin the project than vague notions of 'creativity'.

This chapter then will address the issue of justifying the arts. The first section will consider briefly three examples that use the medium of art itself to provide insight into the value of art. This will be followed by a more analytic discussion of common reasons for justifying the arts and will consider whether there are different ways of looking at the question other than simple providing a list of reasons. Notwithstanding the warnings in this section about making holistic claims, the final section of the chapter will return to the value of a more integrated, holistic perspective.

Insights from art

'I doubt whether I have been quite right in the manner of her education.'

(Dickens, 1989: 320)

Towards the end of Dickens' *Hard Times* the main protagonist Gradgrind comes to realise that he has brought his daughter Louisa up in the wrong way. He sees that his obsession with facts, logic and systems has caused her untold damage. In an earlier chapter, Louisa confronts him over her marriage to a much older man, arranged by Gradgrind purely for convenience without regard for his daughter's wishes. She recognises with some poignancy that if she had been allowed to exercise her imagination (or 'fancy') in her earlier life she would have been 'a million times wiser, happier, more loving, more contented, more innocent and human in all good respects' (ibid.: 289). In childhood she had been robbed 'of the immaterial part of my life, the spring and summer of my belief, my refuge from what is sordid and bad in the real things around me ...' (ibid.: 288).

Hard Times embraces a number of themes including, 'the grinding ugliness of industrial development; the abstract theory of Utilitarianism; shallow self-interest; the anti-social force of the capitalist; and trade unionism' (Hobsbaum, 1972: 174). It also addresses the theme of education; Gradgrind's narrow obsession with 'fact, and of nothing but fact' (Dickens, 1989: 9) has been frequently quoted in writing about teaching almost to the point of cliché. What is less often referenced is the contrasting vision in the novel embodied in the circus characters related to 'fancy', entertainment, education of feeling and sensibility. Perhaps the choice of circus rather than high art as a metaphor for the contrasting world view did not induce contemporary critics to make the connection with art. The circus symbolises the importance of 'amusement' interpreted in its deepest sense. When Gradgrind sees his children trying to peep through a hole to see the circus he compares it to reading poetry as a pointless activity. The effect of the limitation of imagination is seen in the dysfunctional life of Louisa and even more so in that of Gradgrind's son Tom. It is not too far-fetched to read the novel as an implicit justification for the importance of artistic activity for an enriched life.

Art deals in particulars. In as much as individual works of art themselves provide specific insight into the value of art, they do so not through logical, discursive argument but through symbolic meaning and appeals to intuition; they work more through 'showing' rather than 'saying'. That does not mean they are immune from criticism. Some readers might find Dickens' vision in *Hard Times* excessively romantic and sentimental. However, for those for whom the contrast between head and heart, between 'educating the reason' and 'cultivation of the sentiments and affections' (ibid.: 64) as presented in the novel, rings true, the holistic vision will be convincing.

Further insight into the nature of art is provided by two paintings produced by Matisse on the theme of dance. Both depict five naked dancers in vivid colours. In one (Hermitage Museum, St Petersburg) the whirling bodies stand out in vivid red against the green and blue of the earth and sky. The five dancers are drawn in a 'deliberately gauche and childish way' that resembles 'some tribal carving or neolithic fertility idol' (Jones, 2008: 22). The painting thus 'reconnects jaded modern eyes with the primal origins of art' (ibid.: 22). The simple lack of background reinforces the ethereal nature of the painting and the joy in dancing for its own sake. The fact that the dance is being celebrated in another art form extends its sphere of reference to art more generally. The dancers are holding hands in a circle underlining the communal nature of art. As with *Hard Times*, not everyone will necessarily agree with such opinions. In 1910 Matisse was confronted with an almost unanimously negative critical response (Foster *et al.*, 2004: 100). We do not of course have to accept what others say but there is every chance that our response to art will be enhanced by a variety of opinions and responses. The role of the critic and commentator has often been insufficiently addressed in arts in education.

The value of art, in this case music, is also voiced in the final act of *The Merchant of Venice* when Lorenzo declares that

> The man that hath no music in himself,
> Nor is moved with concord of sweet sounds
> Is fit for treasons, stratagems and spoils;
> The motions of his spirit are dull as night,
> And his affections dark as Erebus:
> Let no such man be trusted. Mark the music.

(V, I, 83–88)

Tilghman (1991: vii) begins the preface to his *Wittgenstein, Ethics and Aesthetics* with this quotation but goes on to say that although he knows deep down that this is 'but a poetical conceit', he would nevertheless like to believe that it is true not just of music but the arts generally. He also acknowledges that there are too many counter-examples that can be quoted to be convinced by such a bold declaration of the link between appreciation in art and moral character. Literary expressions of this kind that seek to capture the value of art may not be able to withstand the application of cold rationale and logic but that is to miss the point; the expression, though not impervious to contradiction, still has impact and power. However, such literary conceits and appeals to personal experience are not intended to replace a more discursive, analytic approach to justifying the arts which needs to be considered.

Approaches to justifying the arts

The question 'why should we teach the arts?' is one that advocates of the arts are often asked to consider and address. It seems simple enough on the surface but is in fact deceptively complex. A series of reasons justifying the inclusion of the arts in the curriculum can be provided fairly easily, and much polemical writing on arts education has responded to the challenge in that way. However, the reasons that are advanced often appear superficial if they are presented simply as bald statements, and unconvincing if the claims are excessive. It is important to distinguish between advocacy on the one hand and a quest for understanding on the other. Advocacy involves tactical judgements that are inevitably formulated in the context of current political and policy priorities. When asked to justify the arts in a hostile context, arguments that are influenced by the prevailing climate are often highly defensive. For example, much of the writing on the arts in education in the 1980s was set against a background of a back-to-basics movement when the arts were in considerable danger of marginalisation in schools. There was increasing emphasis on basic skills to ensure economic success. Under those circumstances it was understandable that some arts advocates chose to emphasise the contribution the arts make to employment, the economy or academic success in other subjects. Ross (1984) took issue with those who, through expediency, emphasised the 'academic' and the 'instrumental' value of art education. He referred to the academic curriculum as that which introduced children to the world of 'pure knowledge and to the rewards of scholarship' (ibid.: vii), whereas using art in an instrumental way was to use it primarily as a 'pedagogic device' (ibid.: ix). These have continued to be controversial issues. In the twenty-first century, arts and creative activity in general have been justified in relation to desirable social outcomes. Neelands and Choe (2010) have examined ways in which ideas of creativity have been used to respond to social-political and economic agendas. One of the major success claims of the Creative Partnerships initiative in the UK was that it contributed so much to the economy (Ward, 2010).

One common response to the question 'why should we teach the arts?' is to produce a series of reasons, as in the following list:

- provide enjoyment and pleasure;
- improve performance in other subjects;
- provide future audiences;
- develop the mind – help pupils to think;
- provide future artists;
- develop personal qualities;
- develop imagination and creativity;
- provide insight into human situations;
- educate the emotions;
- develop physical qualities.

This seems logical enough but problems are quickly revealed if the list is probed in more detail. It is revealing for example if attempts are made to (i) exclude any items because of disagreement, (ii) prioritise them from the most to least important, or (iii) identify any missing items.

There are a number of contenders for exclusion from the list. Many writers specifically deny that a central aim of art education is 'to provide enjoyment and pleasure', arguing that the notion of pleasure trivialises the arts. They point out that other activities such as eating sweets or playing games can just as easily provide pleasure. Broudy (1991: 128) was concerned to dispel the view that 'arts programs are forms of pleasant entertainment or hobbies – a relief from the so-called basics rather than a part of them'. The arts must not be seen merely as 'an unjustifiable and humanist pleasure that exists only for the sake of those who enjoy them' but rather as necessary for human development and innovation (Rolling, 2008: 2). Tolstoy (1995: 35) was emphatic that it was wrong to focus on 'beauty, or that which pleases us' as the basis for defining art. These sentiments are worth bearing in mind the next time we are tempted to justify arts activities on the grounds that the children 'really seemed to have a good time'. On the other hand, not to recognise pleasure as an appropriate aim seems rather po-faced and puritanical.

Similarly 'improve performance in other subjects' seems the ultimate extrinsic, instrumental reason for teaching the arts and thus to some may be a strong candidate for exclusion. As a form of advocacy it is very defensive; after all, there are few attempts to justify maths on the basis that it improves performance in music (although such arguments could be mounted). A highly extrinsic reason of this kind is also unhelpful as a focus for advancing understanding because it directs attention away from art forms and processes. The phrase itself 'improve performance in other subjects' is ambiguous. It may refer to the claim that exposure to the arts has a direct effect on cognitive performance elsewhere as in the case of music and maths (the research claims for this will be examined in Chapter 4). Or it may refer to the fact that arts subjects can be used in an integrated way to improve pedagogy and performance (as for example in the use of drama to teach history). In either case the benefit of the arts for other subjects are often seen as a contingent rather than central justification. Sometimes engagement in the arts is seen as a way of developing academic performance because it improves attendance and attitudes to school as a knock-on effect. However, this is better seen as a pleasing by-product rather than a central justification. If a distinction is made between the specific *aims* of arts teaching and the *consequences or benefits* of the arts then this can open up enquiry and discussion without necessarily including the latter as a central justification.

'Provide future artists' may also be thought to be too much of a functional, minority reason for teaching the arts, only serving to reinforce an elitist tendency. In the past, music teaching in schools has suffered from being seen as primarily directed at a select, talented few. It might be argued that arts education should be aimed at the majority, to produce potential consumers rather than artists. This distinction highlights the need to go beyond the bald statements themselves and ask what, if any, are the practical consequences. There is, for example, no indication of what 'provide future audiences' means in relation to classroom practice. Is the implication that the curriculum should be restricted to responding to the works of others? Conversely, does 'develop imagination and creativity' mean that pupils should be primarily engaged in making their own art? One of the problems when statements are listed in such a bald fashion is that there is insufficient detail to discern the concrete implications for teaching the arts.

This lack of transparency in the language of the statements on the list due to a lack of contextual detail can also cause problems when attempts are made to prioritise them. 'Educate the emotions' as a statement on its own is vague when presented in this way. However, it begins to have purchase when it is contrasted with 'develop the mind' because two fairly distinct types of practice can be inferred. One points towards more sensuous, expressive, creative activity, the other to more cerebral critique or discussion.

There is, however, no guarantee that everyone would interpret the statements in the same way. Attempting to prioritise the statements, although made difficult because of the lack of detail, does at least highlight the fact that a very different picture of classroom practice can be envisaged if the balance tips towards one statement rather than another.

Of all the statements on the list, 'develop imagination and creativity' is potentially the most vacuous and uninformative and yet it is often included as one of the commonly quoted reasons for teaching the arts voiced by teachers. In a research project conducted by Downing *et al.* (2003), when headteachers and teachers were asked to tick five most important reasons for teaching arts in their school, the most highly endorsed category was 'to develop creative and thinking skills'. This statement is rather broader that simply 'develop creativity'; by yoking together expressive and cognitive aspects of the arts into one statement a wide range of possibilities is covered without saying very much. It is therefore difficult to know whether the teachers were prioritising 'creativity' or 'problem solving'. It is also difficult to raise any objection. Issues of justification become more interesting when differences in practice are highlighted. A list of comprehensive reasons celebrating the value of the arts may, contrary to the intended outcome, induce tepid agreement rather than passionate commitment. It sometimes helps to group lists in broad categories. At different times in its history the arts have been justified in education in different, and sometimes very narrow, ways as cultural heritage, personal growth, training in functional skills, understanding of the human condition, problem solving and the development of empathy.

No matter how comprehensive a list of reasons is intended to be, other readers are likely to identify missing items. How does the list measure up to some other attempts to justify the arts? One of the specific objectives of the Gulbenkian Report on the arts in schools (Robinson, 1989: xii) was 'to put the case for the arts as clearly as possible to policy-makers at all levels'. Accordingly, it sets out six reasons for including the arts in the curriculum as follows: developing full variety of human intelligence; creative thought and action; education of feeling and sensibility; exploration of values; understanding cultural change and differences; developing physical and perceptual skills. Of these, 'understanding cultural change and differences' and 'exploration of values' do not appear at all on the original list in this chapter and some of the other statements are given a different nuance. Eisner (2002), in his discussion of the cognitive value of the arts, introduces a different kind of phraseology attesting to the value of the arts in helping pupils to: explore new possibilities, tolerate ambiguity, explore what is uncertain, exercise judgement free from prescriptive rules and procedures, develop individual autonomy, inspect more carefully our own ideas and discover the contours of our emotional selves. A cursory glance at a series of websites reveals other contenders: language education, boost reading readiness, help social development, foster positive attitudes towards school. The list could easily be doubled or trebled.

The point of this discussion is not to question the value of listing the benefits of the arts. There are times when polemic is exactly what is required. Also, in due fairness to some of the authors and reports quoted, the list of statements are not always presented in a decontextualised way but are often accompanied by more detailed discussion. However, providing justification can feel more like an exercise in rhetoric than theoretical enquiry, induced more by political necessity than intellectual challenge and without any concrete application to pedagogy. If the value of the arts is not self-evident it is difficult to advance arguments to convince those who have no knowledge or affinity with them. Not that many educationists or policy-makers admit to coming in the latter category. And yet, as indicated in the introduction to this book, the arts are rarely thought by the committed to be taken as seriously as they should be.

A further complication arises in that it is not apparent that all of the statements apply equally to all of the art forms. The aim to 'develop physical qualities' certainly seems to stand out from the others as referring more specifically to dance. However, it is less easily applied to the practice of poetry or indeed to the process of responding to art. The hidden and perhaps unintended implication of the aim 'to develop physical qualities' is that the focus is on creating art rather than responding to work produced by others. The aim 'to provide insight into human situations' seems to apply more readily to the literary arts, although once again a wider sphere of reference can be advanced with a little ingenuity. Whether there is any justification for treating the arts as a composite group will be discussed in more detail in Chapter 9. However, it is sufficient to note here that identifying the problem casts further doubt on whether such lists of statements contribute much to understanding.

Long lists of justifications, then, can obscure theoretical differences and from a tactical point of view in the political arena can appear overblown (Fleming, 2006b). They are well meant but not always helpful. Nor do they go far in explaining the deep importance of the arts in so many people's lives. When a long list of reasons for teaching the arts is taken together they can obscure differences of emphasis in practice. (Questions about justification should not just be about 'why?' but should extend to questions about 'how?'.) It may be helpful to examine some of these key differences in more detail. In each case one possible response is to reject the dichotomy and simply assert that balance is required. However, this does not take understanding very far and is not that different from simply asserting the value of the arts. Three sets of contrasting concepts will be introduced briefly here and addressed in more detail in Chapters 3 and 6.

Dichotomies

Creating/responding

The changing emphasis on 'creating' and 'responding' in the history of arts education is extremely well illuminated by the analysis provided by Abbs (1987, 2003). He points out that the dominant practice in arts teaching up to the 1980s was shaped by the twin influences of progressivism and modernism. The influence of progressivism and child-centred ideas in education meant that priority was given to self-expression and creativity. The teacher was essentially, the releaser of the child's innate creativity. This meant that in practice the emphasis in the classroom was on creating or making art, tending more towards free expression, rather than focusing on responding to the work of others or the acquisition of skills. This was the influence of the progressive strand with theoretical influences coming more from writing in psychology and education than aesthetics and art theory. The direct influence of modernism is more difficult to discern from reading the literature of this period but the consequences Abbs describes are clear, irrespective of the cause. Here the turning away from tradition associated with modernism in the wider society reinforced classroom practice that neglected attention to understanding of form and work produced by others. The alternative paradigm for the arts advanced by Abbs is more inclusive. This view sees a 'reciprocal flow between tradition and innovation, between form and impulse, between the society and the individual, between the four phases of *making, presenting, responding* and *evaluating* which mark the four essential elements of the aesthetic field' (Abbs, 1987: 55).

This view of the development of arts education in terms of two broad paradigms is extremely useful and will be returned to in other chapters. Paradoxically its utility derives in part from its tendency to over-generalise because it gives such an easily accessible handle on over 80 years of arts education practice. There are four qualifications that can be applied to this account, none of which detract from its central value. First, it does not take account sufficiently of a developmental perspective on arts education which sees the curriculum balance between creating and responding changing as pupils get older. This perspective was important to Slade's (1954) view of drama education, although he is often seen as epitomising the creative, self-expression approach. Second, the exponents of arts education writing at the time (Slade on drama, Cizek and Read on visual art) had a more subtle approach than the two-paradigms view attributes to them. Third, the emphasis on self-expression is more easily applied to drama, dance and visual art but much less to music education. This is acknowledged by Abbs (2003: 52). Finally, it is only partially true that the first paradigm has been superseded by another. For example, although there is now a more inclusive approach to the teaching of drama, embracing text, response and theatre tradition, the value of the subject is still often conceived in terms of creating. Despite these caveats, the relative emphasis on 'creating' and 'responding' brought into clear focus by Abbs' analysis can bring greater discrimination to a list of justification statements. For example, when the development of creativity and imagination is offered as a central aim of arts education it is important to consider whether there is particular bias lying behind that formulation and whether it restricts the approach to teaching art.

Feeling/cognition

The contrast between 'head and heart' or 'reason and emotion' found in the Dickens reference near the start of this chapter is one of the traditional distinctions in philosophy that has underpinned much thinking in the arts. Plato objected to poetry and music because they appeal to emotions rather than our intellect. Emotion was central to the expressive theories of Tolstoy, Croce and Collingwood with a different type of emphasis in each case (to be explored more fully in Chapter 2). According to Osborne (1968: 132) the distinction was one of the key aspects of the aesthetics of romanticism with its 'special emphasis on the affective and emotional aspects of experience'. Central to Schiller's vision on aesthetic education in 1745 was the antithesis between nature, including the demand of feeling, and reason which needed to be brought into equilibrium (Schiller, 2004).

The stress on feeling in arts education can be associated with the emphasis on creating and self-expression. In many classrooms this resulted in a stimulus/response approach whereby the teacher's role was to stimulate and liberate the imagination by activating the right emotional buttons. This found its way into the creative-writing lesson where a classic approach was to light a piece of paper and set the students off writing without any other intervention, scaffolding or support for the process. Best (1992: 30) reported on a dance professor who because she accepted the view that any feeling in response to a work of art was equally appropriate felt 'unable to object when some of her students, as their dance performance, sat on the studio floor eating crisps'. Seen in the context of a broad history of arts education (see Chapter 5) the growing emphasis on feeling in the 1950s and 1960s was not surprising because it can be seen as a reaction against the narrow, authoritarian approach that had largely dominated the general curriculum satirised in *Hard Times*.

The view that the arts provide an important balance to an excessive emphasis on reason in schools was given more contemporary expression in the influential Gulbenkian Report in the UK. It saw the arts as being an alternative to academic study and what it termed 'logico-deductive thought' because 'society needs and values more than academic abilities' (Robinson, 1989: 5). That does not mean the cognitive dimension was excluded entirely. On the contrary, according to the report, 'through the emphasis in some teaching on creativity, self-expression and personal development, the arts had become associated with non-intellectual activities' (ibid.: xii). There is an understandable ambivalence in the view that sees the arts as an alternative to traditional academic study but does not want to go too far in neglecting cognition. This concern for balance was captured in some of the language associated with justifying the arts by other writers, for example as 'a distinct way of knowing' (Ross, 1984: 9). The implication here is that cognition was being seen differently from its traditional conception as being purely related to the expression of propositions. The belief that there was a distinct category of understanding – the aesthetic and creative – was also held by writers on curriculum. Hirst (1974) had identified 'literature and fine art' as one of seven distinct forms of knowledge (in contrast to maths, philosophy, physical sciences, human sciences, history, religion) and influenced policy reports. The publication by Her Majesty's Inspectorate, *A View of the Curriculum* (Department of Education and Science, 1980) identified the 'aesthetic and creative' as a key area of experience. Eisner (2002: xi) saw the neglect of cognition in accounts of the goals and content of the arts to have 'put the arts at the rim, rather than at the core, of education'. One of his central concerns was 'to dispel the idea that the arts are somehow intellectually undemanding' (ibid.: xi).

In much of the more contemporary writing then there is a strong impetus to reject the bifurcation of 'cognition' and 'emotion' in favour of a more integrated vision of human existence. However, the separate constructs may still speak to us as broad indicators of emphasis or even metaphors (as in the Dickens extract) and have value in highlighting differences in practice.

Intrinsic/extrinsic

Another approach to the question of justification is to reject the idea that the arts should serve instrumental goals at all by advancing an argument in favour of their intrinsic rewards. Arguments of this kind can be a welcome antidote to long indiscriminate lists but they may be less persuasive in an education context, particularly in a cost/benefit economic climate. They also tend to close down debate that may help understanding and development of practice. It is fairly easy to object to arguments that are clearly extrinsic, for example that studying music improves performance in mathematics. However, Gingell (2000), goes further and suggests that it is a mistake to justify the arts primarily in terms of the contribution they make to our moral and intellectual life. On this basis he suggests that we get a distorted hierarchy: landscape and still-life paintings are 'also-rans' compared with historical works which have more obvious content. Marxist aesthetics elevates Mann over Kafka; Leavis prefers Lawrence to Dickens. We also miss the appeal of certain art forms: to worry about the 'message' of a Ming vase 'is to miss its aesthetic point' (ibid.: 73). This much is true but it is equally true to say that to ignore the moral content of a Jane Austen novel is also to miss its point. Gingell acknowledges this but his key argument is that the moral message cannot be separated from the art form in which it is embedded. Williams (2002) advances a similar contention in his discussion of whether literature should be used with didactic intent; he too rejects the reductionist use of literature to teach a moral 'truth' but sees no problem in the use of literature to enrich understanding and insight in more open-ended ways. The difference is crucial. As Williams says, much will depend on the manner in which literature is treated by the teacher.

Like all polarities, the extremes, particularly taken out of context, are not in themselves adequate but may illuminate discussion related to justification. The moral view provides a strong account of the place of art in education but is in danger of neglecting form in favour of content and fails to account for particular art forms like music. The intrinsic view is in danger of sounding like mere defiance but in its deeper formulation is seeking to account for the power of art. It is also useful in drawing attention to arguments from biology or nature which a simple list of justification statements often misses. Lyas (1997: 1) gives eloquent expression to that view:

> A child hears a piece of music and reacts by marching up and down, swinging its arms: it listens enraptured to story-tellings: it may begin by simply throwing paint, but soon takes an intense interest in the precise choice and positioning of colours: it delights in the movement of trees and clouds and the textures and fragrances of the world. These responses are a form our life takes, as natural to us as eating and sleeping. They are the beginning of what would issue, were education systems designed to reinforce rather than frustrate our aesthetic development ….

Likewise Eisner (2002) begins his rich account of the role of the arts with the biological features of the human organism, a view also found in Dewey. In the naturalistic view we find a different approach to justification which sees art as an essential part of living.

Art and life

One approach to justification then is to seek a broad encompassing vision of the purpose of the arts in education, although writing in general terms can sometimes appear elusive and indeterminate. The arts in education have been described as a 'value marker' (Broudy, 1991: 132), a 'symbolic system of human understanding' (Goodman, 1976), a 'powerful means of promoting re-creation' (Elliot, 1991: 241), a source for 'intensification and clarification of human experience' (Smith and Simpson, 1991: 14) and 'imaginative cognition' (Efland, 2004b: 751). Such claims out of context can sound vague. However, the arts often deal in forms of understanding which push the limits of language, and any attempt to capture the import of art is worthy of consideration. Wittgenstein (1953: 82) described language as a labyrinth of paths: 'You approach from *one* side and you know your way about; you approach the same place from another side and no longer know your way about'. Justifying art can be explored in different ways from different directions. The previous section of this chapter looked at pairs of concepts as a useful means of getting handle on the need for balance when teaching. On the other hand, broader, inclusive justification may also provide valuable insight because it can seek to account for the deep impact of art in our lives.

The common distinction between the 'aesthetic' (which includes our response to nature) and 'art' (which focuses on that which is intentionally made) is useful in drawing attention to what Tilghman (1991: 91) has called the 'humanity' in art. We can be moved by landscapes, sunsets and cloud formations but we respond to a work of art with the knowledge that human intention and purpose is in evidence. Art is both a fundamental part of life but there also a curious sense in which it is 'not life' in that it brackets or puts a metaphorical frame around particular events, sounds, experiences and holds them 'isolated before us' (Schopenhauer, 1966: 36). I recall many years ago conducting a drama in-service workshop for teachers based on the life story of a homeless person that could be used later with their classes. One of the teachers at the end of the session suggested that instead of the drama it might be a good idea to take the students to visit the Cyrenians (a charity that supported homeless people). She had missed the point about the lesson objectives but she had also missed the point about the art form. Paradoxically it is the 'unreality' of the drama that illuminates life so well. The insight comes from the simplification of experience through focus and selection, through the artistic form to reveal complexity. It also derives from operating in a zone of serious play that has none of the consequences of an equivalent real-life situation.

Wittgenstein (1998: 7) makes the observation that 'The work of art compels us – as one might say – to see it in the *right* perspective' and 'the human gaze has the power of making things precious' (ibid.: 3). Tilghman (1991: 52) similarly suggests that a work of art 'shows us things as seen by someone else' and 'selects an object, a scene, a situation, and makes that object stand still to be contemplated' (ibid.: 54). It is on the basis of insights such as this that Tilghman draws attention to the relationship between aesthetics and ethics, art and life highlighted by a study of Wittgenstein. The word 'contemplation' is one that Wittgenstein uses in this context.

At the beginning of this chapter it was acknowledged that many writers have questioned justifying the arts as 'entertainment'. However, if we replace the word 'entertainment' with alternative near-synonyms such as 'delight' or 'rapture' the idea does not seem so trivial. The notion of 'contemplation' used by Wittgenstein is close to Shusterman's (2003) account of 'entertainment'. To dismiss entertainment and related concepts too readily may be to miss something important. The broad family of words associated with the concept of 'pleasure' range from 'titillation' on the one hand to 'exultation' and 'rapture' on the other. The term 'amusement' derives from the verb 'to muse' whose early meanings are 'to be absorbed in thought' (ibid.: 293). Shusterman goes on to point out that we can associate the concept of entertainment with notions of sustaining, refreshing and deepening concentration; paradoxically to maintain the self one needs also to forget it and look elsewhere. In making space for the concept of entertainment it is not necessary to abandon notions of discrimination, nor are we necessarily forced to elevate the superficial.

Intrinsic arguments represent a holistic/integrated rather than serial/analytic approach to the issue of justification. When they are associated with theories that emphasise the enjoyment to be had from contemplation of pure form they can be associated with a separatist view that removes art from day-to-day life (to be addressed in the next chapter). However, a richer account of the enjoyment to be had from art can relate art to life in deeper ways.

Such considerations that treat art as a general category presuppose that it is possible to say something that is true about the arts as a whole rather than focusing on the different value of the individual art forms. The previous discussion shows that this is possible. However, the very term 'the arts' can also deceive us into making general claims that are unwarranted. It is worth recognising that different art forms and even different works frequently have different intentions and effects; they can enthral, move, enlighten, inform, inspire, amuse, challenge, entertain or provoke. To speak about the impact of the arts as a whole as a generic concept can sometimes be misleading. Asking questions about why we teach the arts presupposes that we know what we mean by the 'arts' – a question that needs to be addressed explicitly in the next chapter.

Further reading

Chapter 4 of Carey's (2005) *What Good Are the Arts* poses the question 'Do the Arts Make Us Better?' and examines critically the ideas of a range of writers from Kingsley and Tolstoy to Gardner and Heaney. As well as Eisner's (2002) *The Arts and the Creation of Mind*, both Dorn's (1999) *Mind in Art* and Efland's (2002) *Art and Cognition* deal with cognition in visual art; see also Efland's (2004a) review of Eisner in *The Journal of Aesthetic Education*. The first chapter of Graham's (2000) *Philosophy of the Arts* addresses art and pleasure including the ideas of Hume, Mill, Kant and Gadamer. Issues related to justification are addressed in Ridley's (2007) guidebook *Nietzsche on Art*. For an evolutionary account of the arts and the aesthetic see Turner (ed.) (2006) *The Artful Mind*. Anthropological and interdisciplinary perspectives on art such as Dissanayake's (2000) *Art and Intimacy: How the Arts Began* open up new insights into the issue of justification. Winston's (2010) *Beauty and Education* presents an argument for a return to the importance of beauty. Cooper (ed.) (1995) *A Companion to Aesthetics* has a helpful entry on Schiller. Shusterman's (2000b) *Pragmatist Aesthetics* discusses Dewey's aesthetic naturalism in the first chapter. For relevant articles on justification see Forrest (2011); Koopman (2005); Lord (1994); Sudano and Sharpham (1981); Mortimer (2000).

2

Theories and definitions of art

Introduction

As part of a research project, one hundred 13-year-old students from a mixed comprehensive school were asked to say which of the following list of activities count as 'art' and which are 'not art'. Before continuing, readers might like to do the same.

- theatre
- television
- football
- cooking
- fashion
- films
- sculpture
- graffiti
- photography
- ballet
- disco dancing.

In their combined responses, photography was the activity most frequently classed as 'art', with theatre a close second. Their first choice is interesting given that some notable writers have questioned photography's status as a representational art (Croce, 1992; Scruton, 2008). Disco dancing, television and football were least frequently classed as 'art', the students making such comments as:

> It doesn't really make you think ... it doesn't look pretty like ballet ... art is something you learn to do ... it has passion behind it and I am not convinced that television does ... I think they are all arts depending on what people like ... it is not art because you can't express yourself.

Some of these brief comments point to polarities addressed in the previous chapter (between for example cognition and emotion) as well as embryonic theories of art related to self-expression and aesthetic form. It is interesting that television was classed as 'not art' by so many students, suggesting that many of them may subscribe to a high-art / low-art distinction. Although, it could be argued that placing television on the list was somewhat misleading in that television is a medium that displays art (plays and films) but is not an art form in itself. Some students took a very inclusive view, 'they are all arts', while others were more discriminating. In response to a question related to the relative merits of soap opera and Shakespeare they commented, '*Eastenders* doesn't teach us anything ... there are loads of common people in *Eastenders* ... Shakespeare is more educational ... Shakespeare is more inspirational'. Discussing the general concept of 'art' with young people in this way can be informative but also can be difficult until some common understanding of terms is established; 'art' often just means visual art or painting. Other diverse uses make the concept of 'art' challenging and difficult to pin down.

In popular usage the term 'art' is sometimes used in a normative or evaluative way just to mean 'good art' – an honorific title. When someone says 'that is not art' they often mean 'that is not good enough to be called art'. Some theories of art do the same. Tolstoy (1995), for example, was concerned to establish the criteria for good art at the same time as he sought to define art. Similarly, accounts that stress the organic unity in art often see this as a defining characteristic, meaning that if the different elements do not unite smoothly it cannot be called art (Weitz, 1956: 29). Most contemporary writers on art theory employ a more neutral use of the term and treat the challenge of distinguishing good and bad art as a separate discussion.

The distinction between concepts of 'art' and 'aesthetic' can also be confusing. According to Lyas (1997: 11) 'we can be immersed in the aesthetic in ways that don't need the term "art" at all'. When we choose a handbag to go with a pair of shoes or a new settee to suit the colour and shape of a room we are making aesthetic decisions. The concept of the aesthetic, therefore, is both broader and narrower than that of art. It is broader in the sense that many writers believed we can have an aesthetic experience in response to nature, e.g. a sunset, but the term 'art' is usually retained for that which is actually made (Hegel, 2004: 3). In this example the contrast is between an *experience* and an *object* which further complicates the distinction. The question of how, if at all, we might distinguish an aesthetic from an everyday experience remains. On the other hand, the term 'aesthetic' can also be seen as narrower than 'art' in the sense that the 'aesthetic' usually refers to formal properties of the art object, the colours lines, structures, rhythms rather than its subject matter or content. Although formal properties of this kind have been important through the history of art, the term 'aesthetic' itself is of fairly recent origin and was first coined by Alexander Baumgarten in the mid-eighteenth century and later refined through the theorising of Kant (Guyer, 2004). Under their influence this narrow notion of the aesthetic led to a narrow account of art and its role in our lives.

Another challenge in trying to define art is that the concept of 'art' is not static but changes over time. It is easy to assume that the group of activities referred to as the 'arts' represents a historical and universal consensus, but it is more recent and more arbitrary than is often assumed (Hanfling, 1992: 7). In his publication of 1746, Batteux (1997) distinguished fine arts (when nature is imitated for pure pleasure) from mechanical arts (when nature is used for practical purposes). In the category of fine art he placed music, poetry, painting, sculpture and the art of gesture or dance, and those have traditionally been seen as central to art education. Amongst the mechanical arts he included such items as carpentry and shoemaking. The distinction he made between intrinsic worth and utility (introduced in the previous chapter) has had a long-lasting influence on theories of art. Interestingly, Batteux included a third category of arts that are both 'useful and agreeable' which he called 'eloquence' and 'architecture', recognising, even at that time, that the strict division was not universally applicable (Batteux, 1997: 104). Changes in the use of 'art' over time are compounded by issues of translation. The Greek word *techne*, which is usually translated as 'art', embraced a wider variety of activities including crafts and the operation of skill or technique (Hanfling, 1992: 5). The wider use of the term is still reflected in modern usage when we speak of about 'the art of joinery' and so on. It becomes very difficult to offer a meaning or definition of 'art' that applies to all cases.

In contemporary theory the attempt to arrive at a precise definition that offers necessary and sufficient conditions for the use of the term 'art' has largely been abandoned. A seminal paper by Weitz in 1956 strongly influenced by Wittgenstein's thinking on language marked a significant change from a search for essentialist definitions of 'art'. Not only did this quest represent a misunderstanding of the way language has meaning but it also failed to recognise that the concept is fluid and changing. The attempt to formulate a strict definition that rules some items in and others out was seen as misguided. Weitz (1956: 27) noted that the traditional view set one theory of art against another, each claiming to be true, 'Even today, almost everyone interested in aesthetic matters is still deeply wedded to the hope that the correct theory of art is forthcoming'. However, he argued that as an all-embracing explanation of art, all the theories prove to be inadequate in some way. He concluded that 'aesthetic theory is a logically vain attempt to define what cannot be defined' (ibid.: 30). Drawing on Wittgenstein's notion of family resemblance he saw no properties common to all uses of the term 'art' but rather strands of similarities. This view accounted for the fact that 'art' is an open concept in that new cases have constantly arisen and will undoubtedly constantly arise. Weitz was writing in the 1950s soon after the notion of 'abstract expressionism' had come to the fore (Foster *et al.*, 2004). His approach then was influenced both by current philosophical thinking (Wittgenstein's *Philosophical Investigations* had been published in 1953) and by the changing nature of art.

In contemporary society new possibilities in art are opened up by new technologies, although as Webster (2007: 1306) points out, 'teachers need to think about how best to assume a critical perspective to explore the implications of the characteristics of new media for arts education settings'. This means rejecting 'technological determinism' which assumes that qualities inherent in the new media are responsible for changes in social and cultural practices and for transforming society and its education systems. He suggests that 'ultimately it is arts educators who have a large role to play in helping children deal with the challenge of the digital world' (ibid.: 1307). Just as the advent of film brought new forms of art, modern technology is impacting on arts education practice, for example in the use of paint programs and animation tools, manipulation of images and digital composing of music, and through easy access to museums and art works around the world.

Weitz's view also had implications for how theory itself should be viewed and how it should be valued. Theories which were often interpreted as attempts to say precisely what art is could now be largely seen as tools to illuminate discussion rather than attempts to provide definitive explanations. The post-Wittgenstein view that the meaning of a term like 'art' is not static but a function of its use in social contexts is compelling. It

TABLE 2.1 Theoretical approaches to defining art

FOCUS OF ATTENTION	THEORETICAL PERSPECTIVE
Artist	Self-expression
	Intention
	Expression (1)
Art object	Representation
	Form
	Expression (2)
Audience/viewer	Aesthetic experience
	Aesthetic attitude
Context	Institutional
	Cultural theories

avoids the trap of assuming that 'art' can mean anything anyone wants it to mean but it also acknowledges that the concept of 'art' is open, evolving and dynamic. According to Weitz, the key question becomes not 'what is art?' but 'how does the term art function in the language?' As he says, 'The role of theory is not to define anything … it teaches us what to look for and how to look at it …' (ibid.: 35). This provides a helpful clue to applying notions of art to education in that a key question becomes, 'how does seeing art in this or that way influence the teaching of art?'

This perspective will be useful when considering some of the major theories of art in the rest of this chapter. They will be examined not as competing attempts to define art but rather as sources of understanding, particularly with regard to art education. Eaton (1988: 6) has suggested a useful way of gaining a broad succinct overview of art theories. Any art situation usually involves four components: (1) the maker or artist; (2) the art object itself; (3) the viewer, reader or audience; and (4) the wider context. Aesthetic theories often place emphasis on one of these four elements more than the others, or upon ways in which these elements interact. Similarly, Hagberg (1995: 6) in his *Art as Language* devotes different chapters to different components (viewer, creator and art object) concentrating particularly on the different focus of attention when we try to account for meaning in art. The overview presented in Table 2.1 is a summary but also a simplification, because the different theories or explanations are not discrete. For example, although formalist theorists focused on the art object, one of their key concerns was to account for how emotion was evoked in the audience or viewer. Similarly, as Kieran (2005: 7) has pointed out, the importance of the 'original' and 'originality' (which seems to focus just on the art object) 'is tied up with the Romantic idealisation of the artist'. The focus of attention on one aspect (whether artist, art object or viewer) does not mean total exclusion of the others. The table is nevertheless useful as an approximate guide as long as its limitations are recognised.

Representation

As with a number of concepts related to the arts, 'representation' seems fairly straightforward on the surface but when probed a little more deeply proves to be rather more complex. Its meaning is easier to convey through examples than through a simple definition. As a total account of art it does not work because it is hardly applicable to music, but how does it fare otherwise? The account by Charlton (1970: 54) begins fairly simply, 'Many works of art are representations. Picture galleries containing pictures painted before 1900 are full of them'. The classic case of representation then would be when a painter sits before a subject or scene and faithfully tries to capture it on canvas. However, Charlton goes on to say that 'plays and works of literature also seem to be representations *of a sort*' (my italics). The ambivalence here relates to the fact that the characters in plays and works of literature do not have to correspond to actual people for them to be seen as representational. The same qualification can be applied to the visual arts. Many paintings are of actual historical or contemporary people but some are not and this does not stop them being referred to as representational. Reid (1969: 96) expresses similar ambivalence when he says that 'poetry and some of the visual arts are clearly "representative" *in some sense of that word*' (my italics). The concept of representation hinges on the relationship between the work of art and reality but not in a simplistic way.

It is helpful to examine 'representation' in relation to other concepts such as 'imitation', 'copying' and 'illusion'. Plato thought of representation as imitation and the concept of 'mimesis' has been used to explain the power of art in education (Cannatella, 2008). Imitation is clearly important to art and life generally. It is an important source of learning. According to McGilchrist (2009: 248) it is a human characteristic that 'is arguably the ultimately most important human skill, a critical development in the evolution of the human brain'. However, imitation is not helpful as a *general* account of art. It does not include all the art forms. As indicated above, music is not included except in minor ways, as in operatic storm music (Charlton, 1970). According to Lyas (1997: 38) it may also lead to a naïve concept of art:

> Think of obvious cases of imitation: you have an odd gait and I follow you, imitating your walk; Percy Edwards could imitate to perfection the flutings of the nightingale. Little of art has to do with imitation in this sense.

An artist in the creative process will always make a selection of some kind, focusing on some aspects more than others even if not always fully conscious of doing so. Of course, much hinges on the way words are used. It is possible to make a similar point by defining 'mimesis' or 'imitation' as being different from mere 'copying'.

Many writers subscribe to a richer concept of 'mimesis' (Rollins, 2001; Cannatella, 2008). Even the very earliest art objects do not appear to be just copying reality. There is some uncertainty as to the role the statuette Venus of Willendorf played in primitive society but many commentators view the exaggerated size of the breasts and abdomen not as a primitive failure to represent accurately but as a depiction of what was important to the society, perhaps a fertility symbol (Spivey, 2005). For the same reason, very young children draw people with a large head with the rest of the body having much less importance. The child, like the artist, picks out and 'attends to certain aspects and not others' (Reid, 1969: 98). Nor is the purpose of art to create an illusion, to convince the observer that what is depicted is real. In the case of *trompe l'oeil* paintings, which do seem to aim to deceive, the satisfaction in viewing the work is in realising the momentary deception.

Representation is clearly an important element which provides a partial account for the appeal of much art; people like to have recognisable pictures of country scenes on their wall; a strong appeal of naturalistic drama is that it appears to replicate real life. However, as a theory it becomes misleading as a source of understanding if it directs attention unduly away from the art work and towards the real or imagined object that the work is supposed to represent. The simple likeness of a representation to its subject plays a very small part of the total enjoyment of art (Reid, 1969: 97). The distinction here is quite subtle; when we look at Holbein's portrait of Henry the Eighth, the subject himself is of considerable significance but the painting is more than a transparent window to the real Henry the Eighth – it is in some way interpretive. There are parallels here between Wittgenstein's early and later philosophies of language. In the *Tractatus* he saw the meaning of language as residing in an isomorphic (one-to-one) relationship between language and reality. In the *Philosophical Investigations*, in contrast, he saw meaning as a function of use of language in particular contexts. Representation needs to be seen as 're-presenting', as transformational, as a process of making meaning, not as a simple process of making a copy.

There are implications in this account for art education. Part of the process of acquiring what Bourdieu (1984: 65) refers to as 'cultural competence' is learning that the degree to which a work of art resembles reality is not necessarily its most important characteristic. This is clearly true of visual art but also applies to drama. Exposure to naturalistic forms of drama on television (e.g. soap operas) may induce participants to assume that the aim is to replicate the real world as accurately as possible when students are creating drama. Thus a teacher's instincts might be to want to perfect the miming of opening of doors, the drinking of tea, the counting of money. This is a complex issue because sometimes it is appropriate to focus on getting the action right but far less often than newcomers to the subject assume. However, the action of the drama needs to be subordinate to the meaning and content (Fleming, 2011a). Thus to begin a simple exchange in an improvised drama between a husband and wife who are worried about their teenage child and subtly inclined to blame each other for her wayward activities, it is not necessary to work out exactly how the mother will pour the tea into the teacup. It may be appropriate, however, to have the mother ironing while she speaks in order to symbolise the gender roles occupied in the household. As Kieran (2005: 147) has pointed out in relation to visual art, 'Far from mirroring nature, art helps us to *make* the visual world for us' (my italics). Similarly it can 'cultivate insight, understanding and ways of seeing the world' (ibid.: 100).

As part of their growing artistic maturity and competence, students need to know when it is appropriate and when it is not to criticise a work by saying that aspects of it are 'unrealistic' or 'far-fetched'. This is not a matter of acquiring general rules but of gaining experience through exposure to a range of particular works and styles and being guided by sensitive teaching.

The development of pupils' understanding and response to visual works that are not obviously 'representational' takes time and focused teaching. Cox (2000), in an analysis of one primary teacher's approach to teaching art demonstrates the important of context and metacognition. The teacher was committed to teaching primary-age children about the work of other artists, and her approach is characterised by sustained periods of concentration on selected works, intense questioning of the children, engaging them in dialogue, providing a certain amount of contextual information, encouraging them to consider multiple meanings and asking them to explain and justify their readings (ibid.: 58). In one example the children were comparing Vermeer's *The Love Letter* with Van Gogh's *Starry Night*. One pupil in his comment thought the Vermeer, in contrast to the Van Gogh, captured a particular moment in time: 'it was as if the Vermeer was too literal to provide the kind of meaning he wanted' (ibid.: 59):

> I'd say with that [the Van Gogh] – that one's free. It can go anywhere – it looks like it can go anywhere. It can be painted as big as it wants to be – whereas that one there [the Vermeer] – it's just like – caught – in just one thing. It's not wild or anything. Like a glimpse of something just to look at – it's like looking through that door and seeing a diary. The thing is that's not going to be everlasting, that position [the Vermeer] whereas that could be, that one [the Van Gogh]. That looks – the sky is going to stay similar all the time, but that's – them people are going to move, so that's why it's just like – caught – in one position, all the time – but that looks like it'll move.
>
> (Ibid.: 59)

Form

The most extreme version of the formalist theory of art is usually associated with Clive Bell. In his view it is the formal properties of an art object (the structure, shape, colour, rhythms) or its 'significant form' that are central to its identity as art. His intention was to identify the one quality without which a work of art cannot exist, thereby searching for the type of essential definition which was later ruled out by Weitz. This emphasis on significant form meant the exclusion of other elements.

> For, to appreciate a work of art we need bring with us nothing from life, no knowledge of its ideas and affairs, no familiarity with its emotions. Art transports us from the world of man's activity to a world of aesthetic exaltation. For a moment we are shut off from human interests; our anticipations and memories are arrested; we are lifted above the stream of life.
>
> (Bell, 1931: 15)

Expressed in this way the case seems to be overstated, but Bell's comment can be understood more easily in context. Bell was writing specifically about visual art. A major aim was to defend the post impressionists, who were not being properly understood at that time. He wanted to highlight the limitations of representation in art which he saw as often a sign of weakness in an artist when content or subject matter took priority over form. Far from ignoring the importance of emotion (as might be inferred from the quotation above), Bell saw art as a constant source of passionate emotion. It is important therefore not to isolate formalist theories completely from ideas related to expression and aesthetic judgement. The disinterested focus on form as a key aesthetic judgement was central to Kant's theory. Although Bell only makes one passing reference to Kant in the preface to his book the two views of art are closely connected.

There is a danger of oversimplifying Kant's views on aesthetics in a brief comment because they are so closely integrated with his wider theories of metaphysics and ethics

(Crawford, 2001; Wicks, 2007). The challenge is compounded by the fact that building a philosophical system is so much less common now and it can be misleading to isolate one or two ideas from his whole corpus of work. However, of central relevance here is Kant's focus on the *disinterested appreciation of form* in the judgement of pure beauty which became a defining criterion for responding to art. Kant sought to detach aesthetic appreciation from other sorts of interest we might have in an object. This view became in turn closely associated with the 'art for art's sake' movement. The previous chapter on justifying the arts contrasted intrinsic arguments with more utilitarian perspectives on the value of art. In the extreme version of the former 'true' art, it is divorced from any didactic, moral or utilitarian function. The concept of the 'aesthetic' associated with formalist theories tended to separate art into a distinct realm apart from life's mainstream – art appreciation became associated with rarefied contemplation of form.

As with representation, formalist theorists cannot provide a complete account of art but they are a helpful reminder of the importance of form, which some writers think has been neglected in the history of the teaching of art. According to Abbs (1989: 37) this resulted in the exclusion of the teaching of technique and convention in some arts subjects. Approaches to dance were criticised because of their psychological, therapeutic orientation rather than a more formal and aesthetic conception of the subject (Redfern, 1973). Visual art teaching was challenged because there was 'no insistence on technique, no ordered method of study' (Macdonald, 1970: 345). Daldry (1998: x) claimed that too much drama work with young people 'privileges content over form' and focused on themes such as homelessness, bullying and child abuse rather than an exploration of theatre forms.

In literature teaching, the neglect of form in favour of subject matter or content was in danger of turning literary study into a form of social studies (Gribble, 1973). A thematic approach to English teaching became popular in the 1960s and 1970s and is still prevalent. This method had the advantage of relating the work to students' experience but ran the risk of circumscribing the meaning of literature by making the text subservient to the theme it served and focusing on content at the expense of form (Fleming and Stevens, 2010: 112). Bell's view, if applied to literature, would result in a teaching emphasis on formal features such as rhyme, rhythm and structure more than thematic content or the moral message of the text. It can thus be associated with the type of new criticism associated with Leavis, manifest in the exercise of practical criticism or close reading (Eagleton, 1983: 43). Herein lies a problem, however. The text in this approach becomes largely divorced from context, including social, historical and ideological considerations that might inform understanding. The teaching may in turn be in danger of becoming mechanistic and arid with insufficient intention to meaning.

> I take a poem, say Owen's *Anthem for Doomed Youth*, and I point out an alliteration in line three. The strong-minded student will ask, 'So what?' For lots of useless poems have alliterations in them. The typical learner, anxious to please, will assume that alliteration is a relevant thing to cite without knowing why. Hence the standard essay when asked to assess a poem, simply lists its alliterations, its litotes, and other such fruit of oxymoronic teaching.
>
> (Lyas, 1997: 12)

The teaching of art can become narrow and restricted in this way if it ignores elements associated with expression theories, the subject of the next section.

Expression

One account of expression that has had a significant influence on the teaching of art is the theory of self-expression. On this view the feelings of the artist are poured forth or expressed in the work and then aroused in the spectator or audience. The arguments against the simple view of self-expression are well established (Hospers, 1969; Wilkinson, 1992). Artists are not necessarily motivated by particular emotions, 'Many specifically deny that they felt happy when they wrote their happiest work' (Eaton, 1988: 25). Using self-expression as a criterion for evaluation does not work because having an emotion in the act of creation does not guarantee the production of art. Moreover, if the work is meant to evoke the same feelings in the audience or spectators the assumption is that all of them will have the same response, which hardly rings true (Hughes, 1993). The self-expression view is primarily associated with Tolstoy, although his vision and purpose were much broader, seeing art as a focus for religious communion. Whereas most accounts of self-expression focused on the individual, Tolstoy emphasised the social dimensions of art.

The influence of self-expression on the teaching of art was reinforced by child-centred, progressive approaches to education (to be explored in Chapter 4) and in its most extreme forms had a number of negative consequences. There were few grounds for evaluating what was produced by children as long as it was self-expressive. There was also an over-emphasis on the creative activity of the students rather than appreciation of the art work of others. The role of the teacher was often diminished to stimulating the emotional response, with little attention to the teaching of form and technique. For these reasons the self-expression view has become an easy target in writing about art education. However, some accounts exaggerate its shortcomings and downplay the positive impact of these ideas when seen as a reaction to the narrow, authoritarian and utilitarian approaches it challenged. There is after all something that rings true with the notion that an artist is *in some sense* engaged in self-expression when creating a work of art. Problems arise, however, if the words are interpreted too literally.

More elaborate versions of expression theories have been developed by other writers. Croce's views on aesthetics are closely tied up with his complex, general philosophy to the extent that modern readers may find the scope of his work 'uncongenial' (Lyas, 1997). However, his writing is significant in highlighting a central dichotomy that has echoes of other accounts of art. Central to this theory is the distinction between intuitive knowledge and intellectual/logical knowledge, which accounts for the difference between a scientific work (analytic) and a work of art (integrated). Intuition which is seen as the ability to form representations to ourselves is also at the foundation of our experience of the world in that it gives knowledge of particulars. It is then our logical capacity which allows us to generalise and form concepts. These representations which we make to ourselves are also expressions and it is in this way that Croce puts expression not only central to the way we make sense of the world but also at the heart of explanations of art. Expression is thus a process of making things clear.

Lyas (1997: 71) provides a helpful example to clarify Croce's use of expression. There is a sense in which when an angry adolescent breaks a window the act can be said to express his anger. This is not what Croce has in mind.

> For now having kicked in the window the youth looks at it and thinks 'the glass is not jagged enough here', and 'the hole should be further over', and makes careful arrangements of the glass until he can say 'that's it! that's how I feel'. That for Croce is how expression works in art. In the first case someone was in the grip of emotion, but in the second the emotion was in his grip because an expression has been found for it, which allows the kind of self-understanding arrived at when one can say '*That's* how I feel'.

Little reference to Croce's work is found in writing about art education and he himself did not write primarily about education, although there is a similarity in some of the themes addressed later by Witkin (1974). However, features of his theory are of considerable relevance to teaching: expression in art cannot be reduced to rules with the implication that it cannot be taught through rules but only through particular examples; the organic unity of content and form highlights the dangers of separating these elements unduly in the classroom; the links between art and life implies a broad rather than elitist approach to teaching art; the distinction between intensity and range offers a valuable criterion for choosing art for study; the challenge to genres provides an implicit warning that an obsession with categorisation can impede the teaching of art. These themes will be revisited in other chapters of this book.

The movement from range to intensity is illustrated in practice by an arts project facilitated by The Forge, an arts organisation in North-East England that works with teachers, youth workers, young people and their families to create arts projects (Forge, 2011). The project began with a range of taster workshops on animation, photography, drama and puppetry so that the participants could choose their own media and focus. They worked on producing an action film and an animation and in order to do so had to develop ideas into a storyboard, decide on the cast and crew needed for the film, run auditions, draw animations, direct, rehearse, shoot and edit the film footage. The resulting products were celebrated in the community. The project gave the girls the incentive to develop their knowledge of the arts in general as they attended theatre performances and went on a cultural trip to London to visit art galleries and museums. The project naturally required the participants to establish trusting relationships with each other, their youth workers and artists. They took a role in defining the 'project rules' (e.g. turning mobile phones off during workshops) and taking responsibility for the direction of the work. The project enabled the young people to explore what belonging to a community meant to them. It thus had a clear social purpose and effect but much of the learning was specifically arts focused (see discussion of *learning in* and *learning through* in Chapter 6).

Collingwood's account of expression is also more sophisticated than crude self-expression theories because it also involves transformation. When a person expresses an emotion, he is aware of

> a perturbation or excitement, which he feels going on within him, but of whose nature he is ignorant. While in this state, all he can say about his emotion is: 'I feel

… I don't know what I feel.' From this helpless and oppressed condition he extri-
cates himself by doing something which we call expressing himself.

(Collingwood, 1938: 109)

Collingwood distinguished art from representation, magic, amusement and most notably from craft. In contrast to the true artist, the craftsman knows exactly what he wants to
make before he makes it.

The expression theory thus incorporated a sharp distinction between the artist,
struggling to body forth a specific emotion in all its inchoate uniqueness and so
unable to rely upon blueprints or received wisdom, and the craftsman, methodically
working towards an independently specifiable product according to tried and tested
principles.

(Mulhall, 1992: 145)

The account given by Croce and Collingwood are both more refined than the self-
expression view of 'having an inner turbulence and then transferring it to an art work'.
Expression theories are valuable in that they draw attention to the importance of emotion
in art which seems self-evidently important. However, they can be criticised because they
tend to look inwards for explanations of emotion in art. Feelings and emotions are of
course internal but the language we use to describe them works externally, pointing
towards a context. We do not distinguish 'indignation' from 'annoyance' by examining
the attendant inner sensation but according to the context, whether for example my car
breaks down because it has run out of petrol or because the garage mechanic failed to fill
the tank (Bedford, 1956: 292). Accounts of teaching art run into trouble if too much
emphasis is given to the internal because this is inevitably hidden and mysterious. (This
point will also be relevant to Chapter 8 on assessment.) As Hospers says, 'To talk about
expression in terms of the artist alone is to miss half the story; no amount of talk about
the artist's inner experiences is enough' (Hospers, 1969: 144). The alternative is not to
embrace a crude form of behaviourism as long as we recognise that people do have
insides, they do have feelings and emotions but the language works outwardly. This
insight also helps to make sense of aesthetic attitude theorists.

Aesthetic attitude

Aesthetic attitude theorists direct attention to the audience or spectator as opposed to the
art object or artist. Here the explanation resides in describing a distinct kind of attitude
which demarcates the aesthetic from other types of experience. Thus the theory often
applies to the contemplation of nature as well as art. Bullough (1912) used the phrase
'psychical distance' to describe the particular attitude appropriate to the contemplation
and appreciation of art. He gives the example of a man who is watching *Othello* but is
unable to focus on the play because he is suspicious that his own wife might be unfaith-
ful. Alternatively, the spectator who is too much taken with the technicalities of the play
could be said to over-distanced. There is no doubt that we do attend to things in different
ways at different times but Dickie (1964: 57) questions the need for a full-blown theory

to describe this fairly obvious fact: 'If "to distance" and "being distanced" simply mean that one's attention is focused, what is the point in introducing new technical terms and speaking as if these terms refer to special kinds of acts and states of consciousness?' I can be distracted from a music performance by people talking behind me but this does not mean that I take up a special attitude when I am actually concentrating. Distance suggests detachment which is hardly representative of the emotional engagement often felt in response to art. There is an argument for saying it is precisely the person who has his own personal difficulties who may be in a position to engage more fully with *Othello*. If he goes too far and jumps on stage to kill Desdemona himself then he has simply missed the fundamental point of drama that it is 'unreal'.

Stolnitz's (1969) version of the theory also tries to establish a stance that is different from everyday experience. He suggests that our normal attitude to things is practically motivated and usually driven by a specific purpose. It thereby tends to select only those features of an object that are useful for promoting or hindering our purposes (ibid.: 18). Aesthetic contemplation, however, is different and does not concern itself with an external goal. He thus draws on Kant's concept of 'disinterested' to define the aesthetic attitude as 'contemplation of any object of awareness whatever, for its own sake alone' (ibid.: 19). Once again the discussion centres on the contrast between practical utility and notions of art and the aesthetic. Kant (1928: 43) described the judgement of taste as independent of all interest in the 'real existence of the thing'; aesthetic attitude generally does not distinguish between art and nature. By rejecting any notion of utility or external purpose it creates an account of art that is separate from normal everyday life. It can thus be closely associated with formalist theories that led to narrow concepts of 'art for art's sake' – a 'separatist' view.

Focusing on the role of the viewer or spectator can be helpful in the context of art education. The rewards we get from art are not always instantaneous and may take time. Students may need to be helped to notice some things rather than others and have their attention directed to particular aspects of an art work. It may also be useful, at the appropriate age, to have pupils reflect on the nature of art and different genres. It is little wonder that students are often bewildered by poetry if they approach it with the expectation that it will yield meaning in the same way as prose (Fleming, 1992). Traditional approaches to the teaching of literature and other art forms directed students to work out the artist's intention and ignored the importance of the free play of the respondent. Response theories have focused on the viewer or spectator role in making meaning and can prevent over-emphasis on the artist's intention as the sole authority.

Context

As described, theories of art have historically tried to establish criteria for determining what counts as art and what does not. They did so by focusing on aspects such as formal features of the work or the expression of the artist. The more recent institutional theory took a different approach and looked at the wider context. This approach is helpful in drawing attention to the fact that judgements about art and what constitutes art are negotiated within the communities we inhabit. Danto (2004: 28) acknowledged that 'telling artworks from other things is not so simple a matter' but suggested that it was the art-world that was the determining factor. Various versions of the theory were developed by Dickie (1974; 1983) who suggested that a work is classified as art if a group of informed people confer the status of art upon it. It is the artworld that maintains the category of art in the wider cultural context.

The institutional theory has been criticised as being circular but is valuable in drawing attention to the fact that art exists in wider social contexts and that understanding of art needs a wider vision that takes account of ideology, economics and class. The other theories of art examined in this chapter have some value in contributing to our understanding of art and specifically art in education but they are, like the concept of the aesthetic itself, inclined to be separatist. A full understanding of art in the modern world needs to take account of the wider social context which will be addressed in the next chapter, a discussion which will also help to throw more light on the type of responses given by the students at the start of this chapter.

Further reading

Warburton's (2003) *The Art Question* is a clear and informed discussion of theories of art with very telling examples. Similarly, Freeland's (2001) *But Is It Art?* is clear and very engaging. The first section of Hanfling (ed.) (1992) *Philosophical Aesthetics: An Introduction* has several chapters addressing the question 'What Is Art?'. There are chapters on form, expression and aesthetic attitude in Hospers (ed.) (1969) *Introductory Readings in Aesthetics* and entries on artworld, form, representation and expression in Cooper (ed.) (1995) *A Companion to Aesthetics*. There is also a section on 'Identifying Art' in Lamarque and Olsen (eds) (2004b) *Aesthetics and the Philosophy of Art*, which contains some classic papers. Feagin and Maynard's (eds) (1997) *Aesthetics* is also a good collection of extracts with a section on 'Why Identify Anything as Art?'. Eaton has a chapter 'Art and the Aesthetic' in Kivy (ed.) (2004) *The Blackwell Guide to Aesthetics*. Eagleton's (1990) *The Ideology of the Aesthetic* provides the social background and context for the rise of aesthetic discourse. For a reply to Weitz see a paper by Mandelbaum (1965).

3

Influences on teaching the arts

Introduction

The boys in the art class are all concentrating intensely. Each of them holds a piece of chalk in his right hand and is carefully drawing the contours of a leaf. Occasionally they glance up so that they can accurately replicate the example on the board drawn by the master. Each drawing is identical. They are all doing well in the task because they have spent many hours previously copying straight lines and geometric figures on their slates. In another art class the teacher has provided a general subject matter for the work but in this mixed group each individual is painting a personal interpretation in vivid colours. At the back of the class is a display of work from previous lessons, bright, varied, imaginative and rhythmical. These two lessons are summarised from Macdonald's (1970: 352) *The History and Philosophy of Art Education* where they are depicted in photographs. The first, taken in 1901, shows 'Freearm drawing', which was introduced on a national scale in 1895 by 'The Alternative Syllabus of the Department of Science and Art'. The second lesson from c. 1945 came after the introduction of what was called the 'New Art Teaching'. What factors arose in the intervening years to influence the change in approach?

The factors that influence the teaching of the arts are not that easy to discern and are related to a convergence of elements at a particular time rather than one single cause. Ideas and practice change as the world changes and this does not necessarily happen primarily through rational debate and theoretical writing. In as much as theory did influence the teaching of the arts, it is generally recognised that for much of the twentieth century this happened more from educational and psychological theories rather than philosophical writing about the arts. Sometimes influences are apparent but not acknowledged. Government policy documents related to arts education in the UK largely did not tend to make much reference to related literature. For example it seems likely that the discussion of art and craft in the Board of Education (1937) *Handbook of Suggestions for Teachers* addresses themes also found in Collingwood's (1938) writing but no such explicit reference is made. A further challenge in drawing general conclusions is that individual arts subjects were prone to different influences. Visual art took heed of developmental ideas in psychology which corresponded with the increasing interest in the stages of development of the drawings of children. A further influence was the increasing recognition of primitive, tribal art as a sensitive rather than crude form of expression such that child art started to be taken more seriously (Macdonald, 1970: 320). Dance owed its development in the first part of the twentieth century to key individuals such as Sharp, Duncan, Jacques-Delcroze and Laban. Drama was influenced by theories of play, and recognition of the value of dramatic playing led to the identification of Child Drama as a distinct art form (Slade, 1954). The development of the different arts subjects will be addressed in more detail in Chapter 9.

Notwithstanding these complexities, it is fairly clear that progressive thinking had a strong influence on arts education. Historians rightly urge caution about making claims about the genealogy of progressivism in that, 'A concept of educational ideas and practices united by certain characteristics was in existence before it was labelled progressive' (Brehony, 2001: 417). Nevertheless the term itself is a useful focus for considering a range of ideas. The first part of this chapter therefore will consider the primary influence of progressivism focusing on Jean Jacques Rousseau and his legacy. Dewey, whose ideas will also be discussed, is often grouped indiscriminately with the earlier progressives and, although some links are clear, his thinking on education and aesthetics can easily be over-simplified through that association. Rather than harking back to early progressivism, the inclusive approach of Dewey can be seen as pointing forward to more recent cultural theory. The discussion of cultural theory will include consideration of contemporary challenges facing teachers of the arts related to issues of high/low art that are brought into focus by postmodern thinking. How far, for example, should relativism influence classroom teaching? The concern in this chapter is not just to trace influences but also to consider how they can inform understanding of practice. Just like the definition of 'art', what we mean by 'teaching' the arts is not straightforward. Does it mean primarily teaching children to make art? Or teaching pupils to appreciate art (in which case do we just mean so-called 'high' art), or teaching how to think about art – reflecting on the role of art in society? To what degree and at what age should technique and form be specifically taught? How might/do teachers unwittingly damage pupils' engagement and enjoyment of art?

Progressivism

The term 'progressive' can just mean 'being committed to change' as when political groups with different ideologies all claim to be the progressive party. In the context of education the term is sometimes interchanged with 'liberal' or 'child-centred'. It is often therefore employed fairly loosely in modern usage to apply to a range of beliefs about such issues as discipline, homework, uniform and pupil choice. In the 1960s and 1970s progressive ideas in education were widely blamed for 'low economic productivity, immorality among the young, and the decline of academic standards' often without any deep understanding of what progressivism meant (Reese, 2001: 1). It was often defined in relation to what it stood against rather than in terms of what it stood for, in that it was seen by its supporters to challenge the traditional practice of didactic and mechanical teaching based on fear, authority, compulsion and obedience. By its opponents it was seen as a movement that abandoned standards and discipline. Disputes between supporters of traditional and progressive ideas in education have often been unproductive with advocates of one approach exaggerating the defects of the opposition. It is easy to feel a bit weary and jaded about such arguments. However, an examination of its historical origins in relation to concepts of human nature, expression, childhood and epistemology can provide a deeper understanding of progressive thinking and its influence on arts education.

Rousseau's ideas on education are closely associated with his general ideas and political philosophy (Curtis and Boultwood, 1953: 263). However, it was *Emile*, published in 1762, that expressed his central ideas for education. It describes the ideal upbringing for Emile in four stages through childhood and adolescence with a fifth section devoted to Sophie, Emile's future female companion. Rousseau's starting point is a positive view of human nature and denial of original sin. The child starts life in a pure state with any corruption coming from outside, from so-called civilised society:

> Let us lay it down as an incontrovertible rule that the first impulses of nature are always right; there is no original sin in the human heart, the how and why of the entrance of every vice can be traced.
>
> (Rousseau, 1911: 47)

The child therefore needs to be taught in a way which is not contrary to nature. Rousseau's advice for the upbringing of the young infant included a challenge to the common practice of swaddling in early infancy (binding the hands and feet). Rousseau typically overstated his case, claiming that the country in which children are swaddled 'swarms with the hump-backed, the lame, the bow-legged, the rickety and every kind of deformity' (ibid.: 8). Rousseau's opposition to this practice was intended literally but it can also be seen as symbolic of his general views about freedom, expression and the need to minimise adult interference in favour of natural growth in the education of the child.

> The new-born child needs to stretch and to move his limbs so as to draw them out of the torpor in which, rolled into a ball, they have so long remained .... It seem as if we were afraid he might appear to be alive.
>
> (Ibid.: 8)

Rousseau did not write very explicitly about the arts in *Emile*. He approves of drawing but more to cultivate skill than for the sake of the art itself. He prefers a 'dance in the barn' more than 'a ball in the Opera House' (ibid.: 252). He is happy to including singing and dancing as long as it is a spontaneous expression of joy, 'Nothing can be more absurd than an elderly singing or dancing master frowning upon young people, whose one desire is to laugh' (ibid.: 268). He uses the term 'art' in fairly divergent ways, distinguishing natural arts (which may be carried on by individuals) from industrial and mechanical arts. Medicine is described as an art and does not gain much approval. Sometimes the term 'art' carries overtones of 'artifice' and is juxtaposed with what is natural. Prior to the publication of *Emile*, Rousseau had written an essay in 1750 *Discourse on the Arts and Sciences* in which he had argued that the arts and sciences have not improved humankind. The arts were less 'despotic' than the sciences but more powerful because they spread a 'garland of flowers over the iron chains which weigh men down, snuffing out in them the feeling of liberty for which they appear to have been born' (ibid.: 13).

There are a number of themes in Rousseau that influenced progressive thinking in relation to arts education. The emphasis on nature and natural development meant a diminution of the role of the teacher, 'Childhood has its own methods of seeing, thinking, and feeling. Nothing shows less sense than to try to substitute our own methods for these' (Rousseau, 1911: 54). Similar ideas are reflected much later in Slade's (1954) *Child Drama*, where the teacher was seen as more of a kindly guide who should 'avoid too many fussy, unnecessary suggestions' (ibid.: 131). Practical books which followed made similar observations that the teacher 'should only stick his adult nose into their private world where it is absolutely necessary' (Courtney, 1965: 21). The view that the child should be active rather than passive informed views about learning, and the concern to arouse in the child a sense of the observer is reflected in the emphasis on discovery learning. The concern with freedom symbolised by the unfettered limbs of the infant led to valuing free expression and creativity in art. The structure of *Emile* shows a commitment to the view that the child and adolescent develops through different stages – and that different approaches may be appropriate to each one. This developmental perspective is found in the work of Slade and Read, although it is likely they were also influenced by perspectives from psychology. Through each stage the natural growth of the individual is the main concern. Whereas the traditional approach placed more emphasis on the teacher, the progressives placed the teacher in the background and focused on the child; it can be argued that neither approach attended sufficiently to the object of the learning.

Reese (2001: 3) is one of many writers who has drawn attention to the close association of progressivism and the Romantic movement, and points out that the 'child-centered progressivism was part of a larger humanitarian movement'. The general view that young children should be educated in kindly and natural ways, with a strong emphasis on sensory experience and emotion, was a common theme. Rousseau is sometimes seen as the father of romanticism. What is described as the discovery of the child and childhood owed an enormous debt to the age of Locke and Newton as well as to Rousseau and Wordsworth (ibid.: 5). A strong element of subjectivism was also in evidence. Romantic ideas were in part generated by opposition to the ideals of the Enlightenment and of the society that produced them: emotion dominated over reason. In *Emile* the word 'heart' is used well over three hundred times, reflecting the importance of emotion and feeling in the book. The Romantics too were passionate about subjectivism and the tendency inwards toward introspection.

In the UK, progressive ideas in education started to take hold in the early 1900s with a strong reaction against the excesses of restrictive Victorian approaches. These were evident in some publications, as well as in a small number of schools, but the effect on practice was not widespread. Holmes's (1911) *What Is and What Might Be* contrasted different possibilities from 'the path of mechanical obedience' to 'the path of self-realisation': rote learning should give way to the development of creativity and imagination. The opening sentence of his book, 'The function of education is to further growth', announced clearly the significant emphasis in the progressive approach. Nunn's (1920: 89) *Education: Its Data and First Principles* endorsed the significance of a play-based approach to education which was also a strong theme in progressivism. Concepts of creativity, imagination, individualism and personal growth derived from the naturalist view had a considerable influence in Europe in the work of Pestalozzi, Froebel and Montessori.

According to Abbs (1987: 13) the influence of modernist thinking also had an impact on arts teaching. He sees an affinity between modernism and progressivism in that both have 'an orientation to time, a positive forward-looking disposition' (Abbs 1994: 185). This resulted in a neglect of tradition and in the classroom with an emphasis on *creating* art rather than *appreciation*. Meeson (1991: 105) describes a similar influence specifically on the teaching of visual arts, which developed what he describes as 'an anti-historical attitude' that persisted until the late 1960s. This view went hand-in-hand with the idea that art is a natural activity aimed at stimulating spontaneity and originality. Progressivism sought to embrace new methods and found a welcome ally in the modernist rejection of former styles and subject-matter but the combined influence of progressivism and modernism meant a neglect of 'culture, civilization, tradition, form, artifice' (Abbs, 2003: 55).

The rejection of tradition accords with the views of commentators on the individual arts (e.g. Hornbrook on drama, Read on visual art). However, a note of caution is necessary. Read's (1956) *Education Through Art* was first published in 1943 and in the post-war period became a seminal text. It is seen by some commentators as the epitome of progressivism and self-expression in art. Although self-expression was a key element of this thinking, the views given in Read's book are somewhat more balanced than is often suggested. His view of 'appreciation' of others' work is not that it has no place at all but that it is less appropriate for the younger child. He took the view that appreciation 'can undoubtedly be developed by teaching' but that it 'cannot be expected to show itself much before the age of adolescence' (ibid.: 209). In the same way, Slade (1954) is often thought to have been anti-theatre but in fact much of his professional work was in the theatre; he saw performance as coming at the end of a developmental stage and as appropriate for the older child. These writers are not the only ones whose views have been distorted, for the same has happened to Dewey.

Dewey tends to be grouped together with earlier progressives, and in the USA it is often he rather than Rousseau who is described as the father of progressivism. As such his work has come in for criticism and distortion, and has been often 'forgotten, caricatured, or misread' (Fairfield, 2009: 14). His writing on the arts and aesthetics not surprisingly went out of favour with some analytic philosophers because of its pragmatist orientation. Isenberg (1987: 128), for example, acknowledged that Dewey's *Art as Experience* was 'full of profound and stimulating suggestions' but also described it as a 'hodgepodge of conflicting methods and undisciplined speculation'. Isenberg defined philosophical analysis as 'a method of clarifying ideas by revealing their essential constituents' and believed that the way to study something was by 'breaking it up into its parts' (ibid.: 125). In contrast, Dewey's approach was to advance understanding largely by making connections. At various points in *Art as Experience* he challenges various dualisms, for example, between mind and body, soul and matter, spirit and flesh (Dewey, 2005: 23), underpinning an idea central to his views on aesthetics which asserted the connection between art and life. The previous chapter described the 'separatist' tendency in aesthetics, a form of thinking which confined art to a rarefied, detached and elitist realm. In contrast, Dewey, took issue with this 'museum conception of art' (ibid.: 4) or 'compartmental conception of fine art' (ibid.: 6) that sets art on a remote pedestal. In this conception, art is 'cut off from that association with the materials and aims of every other form of human effort' (ibid.: 2).

The more integrated or inclusive view of art developed from Dewey's naturalism. Whereas Rousseau began by asserting the purity of the individual from birth, Dewey's starting point was the basic human organism and its relationship to the environment. Dewey did not equate art with nature but thought that the origins of our artistic lives lie in our natural responses as humans.

> Art is thus prefigured in the very process of living. A bird builds its nest and a beaver its dam when internal organic pressures cooperate with external materials so that the former are fulfilled and the latter are transformed in a satisfying culmination. We may hesitate to apply the word 'art', since we doubt the presence of directive intent. But all deliberation, all conscious intent, grows out of things once performed organically though the interplay of natural energies.
>
> (Ibid.: 25)

Fairfield (2009: 52) refers to Dewey's aim in his general philosophy of education to affect a revolution 'of Copernican proportions' in thinking. That goal required a 'shift in the centre of gravity in education, one that would often be misunderstood by progressivists and others who began to insist on a student-centered conception of education' (ibid.: 52). Whereas some progressives put the child or student at the centre of the education process, Dewey saw the student's *experience* as the key element.

In the context of art, then, Dewey (2005) placed emphasis on aesthetic experience, not just the detached art object. He distinguished between the art product and what he described as 'the actual work of art', which is what the product does with and in experience (ibid.: 1). The artist, art object and viewer/spectator are all important but according to Dewey must be seen in dynamic relationship, not in isolation from each other. The inclusive nature of his views extended to other aspects of his theoretical writing. He asserted the continuity between art and ordinary life, 'art is prefigured in the very process of living' (ibid.: 25), but he does not deny that art and aesthetic emotion is distinctive (ibid.: 81). He recognises the importance of enjoyment in aesthetic response but sees aesthetic understanding as 'distinct from sheer personal enjoyment' (ibid.: 11). It is important to understand 'the connection that art as production and perception and appreciation as enjoyment sustain to each other' (ibid.: 48). His theory is one of expression but he does not diminish the importance of form (ibid.: 118).

What are the implications for teaching art in Dewey's thinking? His views are more subtle than the more extreme child-centred progressivists. While recognising the importance of subjectivity, he did not assert the ascendancy of pure subjective, creative expression over other aspects of art. There is now room for the importance of responding to art as long as this is seen as an active, dynamic process. In this he can be said to anticipate later reader-response and reception theorists (Iser, 1978; Rosenblatt, 1986). Dewey's distinction between *experience* and *an experience* combined with his assertion of the continuity between art and life has implications for the role of the teacher. Whereas the influence of Rousseau diminished the role of the teacher to that of friendly guide, the inference from Dewey's thinking is that the teacher has a significant role in helping pupils respond to art, through making connections with their own lives and experiences. Teaching art is not just a matter of cold analysis of form, nor is it just a matter of learning about art history in a mechanical way, but it is about engaging pupils in dynamic response to art and not assuming that the art object will, so to speak, induce a response by itself. The followers of progressive thinking embraced creativity and self-expression rather more than responding to art partly because it was hard to envisage that responding to art could be engaging, dynamic, creative, or *an experience*. The process of coming to an understanding of art is likened by Dewey to serving an apprenticeship. The teacher's role goes beyond simply extolling the value of art without any sense of how the pupil may be seeing things, 'The understanding of art and of its role in civilisation is not furthered by setting out with eulogies of it nor by occupying ourselves exclusively at the outset with great works of art recognized as such' (ibid.: 9).

Another implication of Dewey's thinking for the teaching of art is the importance given to context. Whereas traditional thinking in aesthetics tended towards decontextualising the art object, the implications of his view are to reach outward. For example, to understand the Parthenon beyond personal enjoyment, one must turn to the cultural context of Athens and the lives of the citizens 'of whose experience the temple was an expression' (ibid.: 3). The inference is that the teaching of art does not have to be confined to a narrow focus on form but can embrace the wider social context. His opposition to putting art on a pedestal did not mean he was against recognition of great art (ibid.: 212); however, he did subscribe to a broadening of the field of aesthetics, rejecting 'invidious distinction among the arts' (ibid.: 195). Dewey sought to understand attitudes to art within the broader social and ideological context; he attributed the rise of museums and the segregation of art from everyday life to the rise of nationalism, imperialism and capitalism. Many of these views are distinctly modern, looking forward to cultural theory, not just echoing the views of earlier progressives.

Cultural theory

Eagleton opens his book *After Theory* with the declaration that 'the golden age of cultural theory is long past and that the pioneering works of Jacque Lacan, Claude Levi-Strauss, Louis Althusser, Roland Barthes and Michael Foucault are several decades behind us' (Eagleton, 2003: 1). If Eagleton is correct then it is all the more difficult to make any claims about the direct influence of cultural theory on the actual practice of teaching the arts in schools. However, given that theory reflects, not just creates, developments in the wider society it is not unreasonable to infer connections. The boundaries between literary theory, cultural theory and theories of art are not clear cut. It is easier to distinguish the traditional, narrow, separatist account of the aesthetic that was developed in the eighteenth century from any similarity with literary and linguistic theories that came later. However, once art is viewed in its wider social, cultural, ideological and political contexts the overlap is apparent. For example, the components of the typical arts situation described by Eaton (1988) in Chapter 2 of this book are similar to Jakobson's (1988) linguistics and poetics model, which was first published in 1960 and highlights the triadic relationship between author, text and respondent. It is not the purpose here to provide a comprehensive overview of cultural theory. Instead the aim is to address some of the central themes that have implications for the teaching of the arts: the dissolution of the term 'art' into 'culture', the notion of art as cultural capital, the erosion of the division between high and low art and the challenge of relativism. These issues are all closely related.

Doddington (2010: 579) has helpfully pointed out the irony that 'art's distinctive role in education has been threatened by a recent resurgence of the idea of creativity and its possibilities for pedagogy and the curriculum.' The UK government-commissioned report *All Our Futures* (NACCCE, 1999) argued for the importance of creativity throughout the whole curriculum, not just in the arts. This marked a change in emphasis from the earlier Gulbenkian Report written by the same author, Ken Robinson, where the arts were seen as an important way to balance the emphasis on academic abilities: 'The arts exemplify some of these other capacities – of intuition, creativity, sensibility and practical skills' (Robinson 1989: 5). There was clearly no conscious intention to marginalise the arts in *All Our Futures*, but there was a shift of emphasis to the use of terms 'creative and culture' rather than arts in much of the subsequent educational discourse. The major UK government-sponsored Creative Partnerships initiative which ran from 2004 to 2010 funded programmes intended to inspire schools 'to deliver the curriculum through innovative teaching techniques' and young people 'to challenge themselves in new ways' (Parker and Sefton-Green, 2010). Out of a series of twelve special literature review research monographs commissioned by Creative Partnerships only two have 'art' in the title. The national body designated to oversee the initiative was entitled 'Creativity, Culture and Education' rather than 'arts and education'. It is important not to read too much in to this – it is clear that there is no explicit intention to avoid the term art. After all, the new body came under the aegis of the Arts Council. However, the move to the greater use of terms 'culture' and 'creativity' is certainly worth noting.

If there has been even an unconscious tendency to use the word 'culture' rather than 'art' this may emanate from noble motives, to avoid fostering any hint of elitism through associations with high art and to challenge the assumptions of the 'bland, paternalist cultural establishment of the post-war epoch' (Eagleton, 2003: 28). Of course the term 'culture' as used by Arnold (2006) can itself have elitist overtones suggesting 'high culture'; however, since then it has come to be used in a wider anthropological sense meaning something more like 'way of life lived' (Inglis, 2004: 3). The use of the term 'culture' rather than 'art' is a reflection of wider developments in society. Bennett *et al.* (2005: 7) refer to the view that aesthetics is seen by some as an 'intellectually bankrupt endeavour' and others think that 'the very concept of art has been liquidated by new forms of visual culture, material culture, mass culture, or just plain culture'. Burgin (1986: 204) in *The End of Art Theory* declared that we can no longer just assume that 'art' is somehow 'outside' of other contemporary cultural institutions like the mass media. These views have potential implications for teaching. One is to broaden the curriculum from the traditional canon of 'high art' to include works more representative of contemporary popular culture. The other is to see art practice not as a distinctive object of study but more as 'a way of life', as a means of enlivening pedagogy by making it more imaginative and creative.

What this amounts to is not taking traditional categories and boundaries for granted. The concept of 'taste', for example, as the capacity to evaluate and discriminate between one work and another is often seen as something natural and universal. According to Hume (2002: 12), those who failed to recognise qualities in the art object were suffering from an 'apparent defect or imperfection in the organ'. For Kant a judgement of taste was disinterested and laid claim to universal validity. More contemporary aphorisms such as 'there's no accounting for taste' and 'I know what I like' seem to reinforce the view that a judgement of taste is foundational and somehow 'innocent' or 'pure'. When we say that someone 'has good taste' it is tantamount to endowing them with a superior moral character. However, a key idea in Bourdieu's (1984) thinking is that taste is determined or constructed by the wider social context and in particular social class. Whereas taste is often seen as a natural gift, it is in fact the product of upbringing and education. Art and cultural consumption, therefore, fulfil 'a social function of legitimating social differences' (ibid.: 7).

Taste, then, is not pure but reflects someone's education, social origin and, significantly, economic power; any hierarchy we see in how the arts are grouped reflects a hierarchy of consumers. Aesthetic choices become one way of distinguishing one class from another. People acquire 'cultural capital' and access to cultural codes that induce them to appreciate certain types of art rather than others. Bourdieu's thinking was based on empirical work carried out in 1963 and 1967–68 in France which centred on a large survey carried out with 1217 subjects. He investigated preferences in arts as well as in other consumer areas such as cooking and clothing, and established a very close relationship linking cultural practices to educational capital and social origin (1984: 13). For example, when confronted with a photograph of an old woman's hands, particular groups react differently. The 'culturally most deprived'

> express a more or less conventional emotion or an ethical complicity but never a specifically aesthetic judgment (other than a negative one): Oh she's got terribly deformed hands! … There's one thing I don't get (the left hand) – it's as if her left thumb was about to come away from her hand. Funny way of taking a photo. The old girl must've worked hard. Looks like she's got arthritis.
>
> (Ibid.: 44)

In contrast, those at 'higher levels in the social hierarchy' make more abstract comments, and references to painting, sculpture and literature are more common: 'I find this a very beautiful photograph. It's the very symbol of toil. It puts me in mind of Flaubert's old servant-woman …. That woman's gesture, at once very humble' (Ibid.: 45).

The fact that Bourdieu's empirical work was conducted in France has led some critics to question whether generalisations can be made from his views. In the Preface to the English edition of *Distinction* he acknowledges that some readers might find the book 'very French' and that it can be read as an ethnography of France. Bourdieu goes on, however, to say that it would be a mistake to regard what is said about the social uses of art and culture as 'a collection of Parisian curiosities and frivolities' and he does not want to renounce the ambition of drawing out 'universal propositions' (ibid.: xi). In contrast, when writing about contemporary American society, Carroll (1998: 180) does not think that allegiance to the practice of high art depends strongly on social background and suggests that 'a taste for popular art and an aversion to high art seems to cut across class lines'.

Despite this note of caution about over-generalising, it is possible to speculate on the possible implications of these views for education. The less radical reaction is to acknowledge the links between art consumption and social class, and determine that schools have a duty to provide all pupils with the type of cultural capital that should not be just the preserve of a few. For example, Guillory (1993) when writing about debates over the literary canon has argued that canon formation should be understood as a question of the distribution of cultural capital in schools. There should be universal access to canonical texts. In pursuit of this goal, Bourdieu's notion of cultural competence may be useful. Mastery is not acquired simply by contact with art. Some pupils, because of their social background, come to school pre-disposed to respond to works in certain ways but it is a school's duty to make sure all pupils acquire the necessary competence to do so. The more radical reaction is to acknowledge that response to art is largely a matter of social snobbery and to abandon any notion of hierarchy between high and low art when deciding what to teach. This view needs further consideration.

High and low art

What is meant by the categories 'high' art and 'low' art? As Fisher (2001: 409) observes, the terms evoke a 'familiar culture divide' which assigns Shakespeare and classical music to one category and soap opera and popular music to the other. The terms are often easy to apply in particular cases but it is not so easy to provide clear general criteria to distinguish them. One possibility is to use 'high art' to delineate 'central cases of art' and 'low art' to refer to works which are not really considered art at all (ibid.: 409). Looking for criteria, then, is really a disguised question about definitions of art. Another possibility is that the terms 'high' and 'low' actually mean 'good' or 'bad' art. The emphasis now is more on value and evaluation, although, as suggested in Chapter 1, this in practice is also often about defining art: when people say 'that is not art' they often mean 'that is not good enough to be counted as art'. The notion of quality is clearly relevant but both attempts to distinguish 'high' art from 'low' offer a spurious clarity which is unproductive. Not only do they beg too many questions (the challenge of defining and evaluating art remain), they make the terms 'high' and 'low' redundant and side-step the interesting challenge of why, in particular cases, the terms can so often be easily applied.

Other attempts to draw clear distinctions between 'high' and 'low' art are illuminating but not conclusive. The idea that 'high' art survives the test of time (Savile, 1982) has some appeal because it covers so many cases but it excludes modernist works and the avant garde, which are often seen as archetypes of high art. The categories themselves may be an oversimplification. In normal usage, categories such as mass art, folk art, pop art, conceptual art and the avant garde are often conflated but distinguishing them highlights further problems in sustaining the distinction between high and low art. Carroll (1998) has provided a convincing defence against the argument that mass art is not genuine art. The concept of mass art is defined by its means of production as 'popular art produced and distributed by mass technology' (ibid.: 3). A film of a Shakespeare play therefore can be seen as a form of high/mass art. Attempts to distinguish the concepts by genre, as with the test of time argument, only go so far. If a ballet or classical music concert is shown on television that does not automatically move it into the category of low art.

Judgements of quality clearly come into the distinction but once again it is not straightforward. One argument is that mass art (as a sub-set of low art) is designed to be easily accessible and therefore does not induce active spectatorship in the audience. This argument is difficult to sustain because how someone responds is less a function of the work itself and more of the individual; reader response and reception theories have stressed the active participation of the respondent in the creation of meaning. Many contemporary television dramas such as *The Wire* or *The West Wing* because they have rapid dialogue and multiple narratives, make demands on the active involvement of the audience. Another view is that mass art is formulaic. But as Carroll argues, all art is formulaic to some degree and the idea that 'artists create *ex nihilo* and that some artists are altogether uniquely independent of traditional modes of composition' is a romantic myth (ibid.: 68).

The word 'art' prompts us into making assumptions about art as a generic concept which are more true of particular art forms. This complicates the process of trying to distinguish high art from low art in any coherent way. A work of fiction may have more content and apparent depth than an abstract painting but that does not mean that it is thereby necessarily superior. Making a simple distinction between 'surface' and 'depth' may be inappropriate and misleading. We do not think a song with lyrics is more sophisticated than one without. Even within music as a genre, classical and rock music may require different criteria for their appreciation and value: 'any attempt to evaluate or understand rock music using traditional aesthetics of music is bound to result in a misunderstanding' (Baugh, 2004: 493) – although that view has been challenged (Davies, 2004). As suggested in Chapter 1, different art forms and works have different intentions and effects; they can enthral, move, enlighten, inspire, amuse, challenge, entertain or provoke. Distinguishing some works as 'high art' may be to apply misleading essentialist criteria to particular cases.

It is little wonder that Carey (2005: 29) sees any attempt at discriminating between art and not art as fruitless and defines a work of art as 'anything that anyone has ever considered a work of art'. While that conclusion is somewhat extreme, it may be appropriate to abandon the analytic search for distinct categories but instead, more pragmatically, seek to understand what the distinction itself means for education. In the context of teaching art, an inclusive approach may be deemed to be more theoretically sound, democratic and pedagogically appropriate. In the classroom, contemporary, popular works can be included which are of more immediate relevance and interest to the pupils. Gingell and Brandon (2000: 415), however, while not wishing to subscribe to a traditional, elitist view, make a telling point about the responsibilities of educators: 'we have to select those aspects of our culture which we wish our children to partake of and insist that our educational establishments make sustained and intentional efforts to ensure such participation'.

Of course ensuring that some canonical works appear in the curriculum does not preclude the inclusion of others. A study by Green (2002) reveals changing attitudes to the content of the music curriculum. Whereas in a 1982 survey it was felt that classical music should take up most of the time on the grounds of its superiority and the fact that students do not have to be taught pop music, by 1998 teachers were more inclined to value a much wider and more inclusive curriculum. There was the suggestion, however, that teaching strategies had not shifted in the same way.

An inclusive approach, however, can easily lead to a purely relativist position. Curriculum decisions are not just about content and ends but also about pedagogy and means. It is one thing to include a variety of different works, but how are these presented and studied? Is popular culture included merely to demonstrate that it is inferior or as a form of tokenism? If not, how do teachers fulfil their responsibility to acknowledge and pass on norms and standards? Is it really justifiable to take up any valuable curriculum time with works which are judged to be inferior? Here, for example, are the views not of a die-hard traditionalist but of a respected writer on arts education in the liberal tradition:

> … popular, shallow, sentimental, cliché-ridden romantic novels, art, and television programmes not only impede an understanding of the human condition, they also contribute to the creation and perpetuation of shallow, sentimental, cliché-ridden feelings. They impede the possible development of genuinely individual feelings: they restrict personal possibilities.
>
> (Best, 1992: 83)

The separatist and inclusive approaches may reflect contrasting positions in the school: on one side cultural elitism, snobbishness, power relations and oppressive hierarchies and on the other side an implicit form of radical relativism which may leave pupils confused and genuinely rootless. Some postmodernist theorists would be comfortable with a relativist position, as would some educators who might evoke radical or critical pedagogy as the practical solution. However, it is questionable whether it is appropriate to be critical without some grounding in norms and standards of judgement.

Relativist thinking takes a broad and complex form and has influenced a number of fields including morality and understanding other cultures. The focus here will remain on art and specifically the teaching of art. Carey (2005) considers a range of arguments and theorists about judgements of art and debunks many traditional views. His arguments about the value of 'low' art like soap operas for so many people are convincing. His final conclusion, however, that 'the absence of any God-given absolutes, together with the impossibility of accessing other people's consciousness prevents us – or should prevent us – from pronouncing on other's people's aesthetic judgements right or wrong' places too much emphasis on subjectivity and not enough on the art object itself (ibid.: 65). Dewey's (2005) emphasis on the interplay between the experience of art and the art object itself makes it perfectly reasonable to say that some works are better than others, which after all makes intuitive sense without resorting to a dry form of objectivism.

Lyas (1997: 128) suggests that the terms subjectivity and objectivity are misleading here. To make a remark about whether one likes a work of art or not is often thought to be the end of the matter. Theoretical problems related to relativism arise if that implicit view is taken. However, according to Lyas, to say that one work is better than another is to 'reach out in an effort to establish community', to invite discussion, to get people to see things as we do'. Concepts of subjectivity and objectivity are simply unhelpful. Judgements about art then need to focus on the particular in this way. Concepts of high art and low art are unhelpful because they over-generalise and have overtones of the class associations identified by Bourdieu. However, the alternative is not to embrace relativism and to assume that every work of art is of equal merit. The concept of 'a great work of art' needs to be retained.

Retaining the distinction between high and low art may have another potentially negative effect on teaching. This is the view that only some works should be subject to analysis and criticism, whereas others are just for relaxation and escapism. As Shusterman (2002: 131) says, popular art 'rewards attentive criticism because it has great aesthetic and social potential, which it realizes in its best works'. He also says that much popular art needs criticism because it needs considerable improvement. It is not helpful to make students feel ashamed or inhibited about their likes and preferences. However, teachers have a duty to help them understand notions of quality, why some works are better than others and to help them explore implicit notions of gender, race and ideology in some of the more popular art works. It is not as if exchanging differences of opinion is alien to young people, whether, for example, the modern band *The Invisible* are better described as indie rock or post rock; why the music of *Lady Gaga* is enhanced by her visual performance; why the group *Abba* were scorned by many contemporary critics and now almost universally lauded; whether *Eminem* is past his best. Such discussions are in the same family as differences of opinion over Shakespeare.

This chapter has focused on an exploration of some of the influences on the teaching of art, which has helped to uncover what 'teaching art' might mean. It must involve more than simply teaching children to express themselves through creating art. Teaching children to appreciate art must involve due attention to both the art object and their experience in relation to it. With regard to content it is reasonable to suggest that pupils should be taught to participate in the cultural world in which they will live with its diverse range of forms and types of art. However, an eclectic approach does not mean avoiding judgements and notions of great art (Arts Council, 2010); teachers are not forced to choose between elitism and relativism. There may also be a case for encouraging pupils to think about more theoretical questions about the nature of art (e.g. why is art valued in society?, what is art?, is all art of equal value?). At what age such an approach might be appropriate is more of an empirical question. The next chapter will focus on the contribution that empirical research has made to understanding the arts in education.

Further reading

The Cambridge Dictionary of Philosophy (Audi, 1999) has short entries on Rousseau and Dewey that provide an overview of their broader thinking on education and society. *The Blackwell Guide to Philosophy of Education* has a chapter on Progressivism by Darling and Nordenbo (2003). For an informed and insightful exploration of high art / popular art and related theoretical issues see the writings of Shusterman including (2000b) *Pragmatist Aesthetic: Living Beauty, Rethinking Art* (2000a) *Performing Live* and (2002) *Surface and*

Depth. Storey's (2001) *Culture Theory and Popular Culture* provides a comprehensive introduction to a range of issues including the 'culture and civilization tradition' related to Arnold and Leavis. *The Polity Reader in Cultural Theory* (Polity, 1994) contains a wide range of chapters by different authors in the field of cultural studies. Klages' (2006) *Literary Theory: A Guide for the Perplexed* provides a clear introduction to this field.

CHAPTER

4

Research perspectives

Introduction

In a wonderfully resonant passage in George Eliot's *Middlemarch* (1994) the author intervenes to pass comment on one of the central characters, Mr Casaubon. He is a rather dull, pedantic scholar who has been working on his life's project the 'Key to All Mythologies', a process of endless cataloguing that is doomed to failure. Despite his weaknesses of character, the author declares that she feels sorry for him and gives her reasons as follows:

> It is an uneasy lot at best, to be what we call highly taught and yet not to enjoy: to be present at this great spectacle of life and never to be liberated from a small hungry shivering self – never to be fully possessed by the glory we behold, never to have our consciousness rapturously transformed into the vividness of a thought, the ardour of a passion, the energy of an action, but always to be scholarly and uninspired, ambitious and timid, scrupulous and dim-sighted.
>
> (Ibid.: 280)

The juxtaposition of words and phrases here is a fitting lead into the present chapter. Whereas art is invariably about transformation, passion and being present at the 'great spectacle of life', research can easily be associated with being 'scholarly and uninspired' and even with becoming 'scrupulous and dim-sighted'. For this reason this chapter is not just about researching the arts but also about research *and* the arts – how different ways of being in and reflecting on the world can easily become associated with these endeavours.

As with other concepts addressed in this book, the meaning of 'research' is not fixed and unambiguous. Nor are the different uses of the term always innocent; they can betray prejudices and entrenched positions. In general use 'research' can just mean 'finding things out'. In the academic world it more often refers to the *systematic* advancement of knowledge but the term may still be ambiguous either in relation to the interpretation of the word 'systematic' or because it can be employed either in a restricted sense or in a much broader way. The term is sometimes used to refer only to empirical research or, more widely, to embrace theoretical or conceptual enquiry as well. Empirical research involves going out and collecting data of some kind through questionnaires, observation, interviews, etc. Theoretical enquiry can be conducted from a desk. Sometimes the term 'scholarship' is used for this type of work with the term 'research' being reserved purely for empirical work. The use of terminology is not unimportant because as with 'art', the term 'research' can be used as an honorific to imply a normative judgement. The notion that 'proper' research is always empirical and 'scientific' may underpin such uses. Within the category of empirical research there are in turn different approaches which have also been the subject of disagreement. This chapter, then, will consider different conceptions of research and the use made of the arts in the research process itself before discussing some of the empirical research on the arts in education. Classic distinctions between science and art, the analytic and synthetic can help elucidate different opinions about what counts as research. Other themes that have already emerged in this book as being important in the discussion of the arts, such as the nature of understanding, the general and particular, the importance of context, the relationship between language and meaning, can also help inform issues related to research.

Ways of seeing

Research in education has been subject to a great deal of criticism, with questions frequently raised about whether the money invested has been well spent. Hargreaves (1996) thought there was little to show for the vast sums of money spent on education research (in 1996 he set this at £50–60 million). He criticised much educational research as being non-cumulative, because 'few researchers seek to create a body of knowledge which is then tested, extended or replaced in some systematic way' (ibid.: 2). In contrast, medical research gives rise to a body of knowledge that more directly influences practitioners. In 1998 the head of OfSTED commissioned a report which challenged the quality of much of the current education research as being inadequate (Tooley and Darby, 1998). The report found that many of the research studies displayed partisanship in the conduct of the research, had shortcomings in methodology and in presenting findings (by putting these in the context of unsupported remarks about political reform), and had weaknesses in argument, including the non-empirical work considered. Hargreaves' criticisms were in turn subject to challenge (Hammersley, 1997) but they had an effect, particularly on policy-makers. Elsewhere, in the USA, Kaestle (1993) wrote an article entitled 'The Awful Reputation of Educational Research' and suggested improvement measures such as greater links with practice, more successful dissemination of results, the design of a more appropriate research agenda. Not all of the criticisms are directly related to theoretical positions. Some of the concerns have to do with the technical quality of the work or with the fact that small studies are fragmented and do not sufficiently contribute to the advancement of knowledge. Nevertheless there are often theoretical assumptions underlying the criticisms related to contrasting views of how research should be conceived.

It is not uncommon for introductory books on research methods in education to describe two distinct paradigms of empirical research. One is described as objective, scientific and positivist, the other subjective, interpretive and naturalistic (Cohen *et al.*, 2007; Opie, 2004). The first is more likely to seek to establish universal rules to determine behaviour through testing hypotheses while the second is more oriented towards establishing how people experience and perceive the world. These two approaches have often been associated respectively with the collection of quantitative or qualitative data, the former involving the collection of data that can be counted and subject to statistical analysis, and the latter involving other data such as interviews, photographs, and descriptions. Alexander (2006: 207) referred to the methodology wars in which 'positivists and anti-positivists of different stripes attempted to expose and defeat one another's assumptions' and suggested that the wars eventually gave way to a truce in which the different camps started to tolerate and even respect each other's positions.

It has been more common in recent years for writers not just to tolerate the divisions but question the false dichotomy they represent, recommending instead 'fitness for purpose' (Pring, 2000; Gough and Elbourne, 2002; Rowbottom and Aiston, 2006). This makes sense. It seems more appropriate to make the choice of research approach dependent on the type of question being asked, rather than on prejudices derived from entrenched theoretical positions. The work of Bourdieu (1984) discussed in the previous chapter demonstrated the value of large-scale quantitative research in describing the relationship of taste to class. Likewise, if we want to know whether engaging with the arts has impact on performance in other subjects, an experimental approach is desirable. On the other hand, there are times when in-depth, qualitative interviews are needed, for example when examining teachers' or pupils' concepts of high and low art. Despite the greater level of tolerance of different methods, some tensions still persist.

One of the persistent criticisms of education research is that it does not deliver clear evidence of 'what works'. Politicians and policy-makers want answers to questions such as, does class size influence achievement, what is the best way to teach reading, is it better to stream or teach in mixed ability groups? Underlying the quest for 'what works' is often an assumption that objective, scientific models that set up experiments, ideally in the form of randomised trials, are required. Oceana and Pring (2008) have described the growing preference amongst politicians in the UK and USA for this kind of research which aims at providing clear answers that can be directly applied to policy. However, the quest for 'scientific' answers, while not in itself wrong, can easily become blinkered. The narrow view that that there is only one sound way of conducting empirical research has already been addressed, but there are other dangers. Such an approach deals in generalities (that is its strength) but in the application of findings may thereby flatten out important contextual differences. Findings about mixed ability are not easily translated from one context to another because they may depend on the social mix and parental attitudes within a particular school. The search for proof based on evidence leaves little room for ambiguity and uncertainty, which are essential elements in fostering understanding; findings need to be seen as contingent and subject to modification with further evidence. Furthermore, such approaches are in danger of failing to recognise the fundamental importance of values in determining priorities in education. For example, empirical research may demonstrate that a particular way of teaching reading raises the level of scores on a reading test but may fail to determine whether pupils are in the process being motivated to read. There is likewise a danger of failing to recognise that language is very often fluid and indeterminate. Experimental research can engage in the rational pursuit of how to teach reading without considering the meaning of 'reading'. These problems arise when it is assumed that methods of causal explanation that operate in the physical world can be easily applied to social science. Ideas related to ambiguity, indeterminacy of language, the importance of the particular and the centrality of values have all been important in the discussion of art. It is little wonder therefore that the contrast between 'science' and 'art' lies behind some of these differences.

So far the word 'science' has been placed in inverted commas to acknowledge that the obsession with narrow logic and rationality without reference to values, and the application of strict rules and methods is not necessarily true science. The word 'scientism' is sometimes employed to capture the kind of misunderstanding and misapplication of science that sees scientific methods as being the only source of knowledge and as having no limits, able to be applied to all areas of human existence. Monk (1999: 66) referred to 'scientism' as 'the view that every intelligible question has either a scientific solution or no solution at all' and Glock (1996: 341) described it as the 'imperialist tendencies of scientific thinking which result from the idea that science is the measure of all things'. The assumption that science makes progress on the basis of the application of universal rules that are strictly logical and rational has been questioned. Feyerabend (1975: 11) argued that there are no useful and universally applicable methodological rules governing the progress of science or the growth of knowledge.

> The history of science, after all, does not just consist of facts and conclusions drawn from facts. It also contains ideas, interpretations of facts, problems created by conflicting interpretations, mistakes and so on. On closer analysis we even find that science knows no 'bare facts' at all but that the 'facts' that enter our knowledge are already viewed in a certain way, and are, therefore, essentially ideational.

Law (2004) has argued that methods are not neutral and transparent; they do not just describe social realities but also create them. The search for absolute clarity and precision in the application of methods is misguided.

The consequence of elevating the status of what is perceived to be scientific method is that it diminishes other ways of understanding the world. This theme is found in a number of twentieth-century writers. Gadamer (2004: xx) begins his *Truth and Method* with the insight that 'the phenomenon of understanding and of the correct interpretation of what has been understood is not a problem specific to the methodology of the human sciences alone' and questions the universal claims of scientific method. His work is particularly relevant because it challenges the failure to see aesthetics and art as a source of knowledge and truth. Notwithstanding intellectual differences with Gadamer, the theme is also found in the writing of Habermas (1987) who too argued against narrow conceptions of knowledge and questioned the dominance of 'instrumental reason'. Wittgenstein was extremely critical of the attempt to transform philosophy into a science and was particularly scornful of any attempt to turn aesthetics into a science (Monk, 1991: 298). He was also highly critical of the idol-worship of science (ibid.: 416).

The challenge to a narrow and reductive application of logic and rationality does not, however, lead inevitably to relativism and subjectivity. Pring (2000: 6) has referred to the kind of discourse that is common in contemporary writing on research which appeals to 'the social construction of knowledge', 'the multiple realities of the learner', 'subjective meanings of the learners' or 'personal construct of truth'. Such phrases are misleading if they embrace relativism and jettison notions of truth. The weakness of this kind of position is revealed by focusing on language, by using Wittgenstein's insight that the meaning of language is determined not *within* but *between* people in social contexts. On this view, meaning is not 'subjective' and knowledge is not 'personal', even though, in as much as it is expressed through language, it is in that sense 'constructed'.

The important point, then, is not to reject any one approach to research as being unable to contribute to the advancement of knowledge but to be aware of the potential for restricted vision. So-called positivist approaches may become insensitive to context, ignoring crucial differences that emerge through attention to the particular, and blind to the potentially misleading effects of language. More interpretive approaches, on the other hand, may be prone to philosophical errors, all too ready to embrace extreme forms of subjectivism and failing to recognise the importance of the pursuit of truth. Being able to see things from different perspectives and being encouraged to notice things is precisely what our involvement in the arts can develop. It is no surprise therefore that the arts are increasingly being used in the process of research itself.

Arts-based research

Interest in arts-based research has grown steadily in the last 30 years. The term is used to refer to the use of arts activities either to collect or to present data. This means also that the concept of 'data' is also widened from a traditional reliance on numbers and propositional statements to a more varied use of language (poetry, narrative) or non-linguistic forms (pictures, dance). Barone and Eisner (1997: 95) refer to the growing numbers of educational scholars and researchers who have explored the enquiry approaches that are 'in varying degrees and ways, artistic in character'. McNiff (1998: 11), writing from a creative arts therapy perspective, asked whether 'we are ready to use our unique methods of artistic enquiry to shape a new vision of research'. Since these publications, there has been a growing number of books and edited collections addressing similar themes (see further reading section).

Dance provides an interesting example of an original and challenging approach to presenting data because of its non-linguistic form. Blumenfeld-Jones (1995: 391) argued for dance as a 'viable representation mode of research' on the grounds that language is not the transparent conveyor of meanings as is often assumed and that 'the focus should be on how dance might extend, energize, and bring out previously unseen aspects of the objects of our interest' (ibid.: 400). Bagley and Cancienne (2001) describe a project which used data collected by one of the partners (interview transcripts of parents of children with special educational needs) as the basis for a dance performance choreographed by the other partner who had a background in the performing arts. The final performance used words as well as movement.

> The purpose of these movements was to bring the text to life in ways that the reading of it could not. [. . .]
> Dance in the performance moves beyond the actual interviews and takes creative license. This is done for purposes of seeing old information in a new light and creating a new interpretation from the old.
>
> (Ibid.: 226–227)

The purpose of the dance interpretation, then, was to lift the experiences and voices of the participants 'off the printed page' and give the text a 'lifelike dimension' (ibid.: 233). The use of a partnership between researcher and dance choreographer (who was also an academic researcher) was an important aspect of this project in avoiding the general criticism that arts-based research may appropriate ideas from art in a superficial way. Another interesting aspect of this project is the mixed use of text and dance in the presentation of the data because this suggests a level of continuity rather than a radical departure from traditional methods. In some of the literature related to arts-based research there has been an element of ambiguity with regard to how this approach is related to other forms of research. McNiff (1998: 13) emphasises the need for art-based research but does not question the value of 'conventional behavioural science methods'; he rather wants to establish a 'respected place for art-based research within the total context of research' and an expansion of assumptions about what research can be. Barone and Eisner (1997: 96) describe traditional research as striving 'towards certainty', whereas arts-based research is the 'enhancement of perspectives'. Underlying these views is a conception of arts-based research as being of a rather different kind, a view that can be questioned.

The concepts of separatist and inclusive approaches to art addressed in this book can also usefully be applied to 'research'. A separatist view emphasises the distinction between traditional and art-based approaches and reinforces the dichotomies referred to earlier in this chapter. On this view one or other approach is superior, depending on one's viewpoint. To many commentators, including some advocates of art-based research, so-called objective methods are different in kind and remain the gold standard. On this view there is often a misconception of what it can and cannot achieve. An inclusive approach, on the other hand, emphasises the similarities in philosophical underpinning and objectives in different approaches to research. Research, of whatever kind, seeks to advance understanding and contribute to the organic growth of knowledge. Emphasising the continuity implies that certain standards of rigour, transparency and convention are applicable and avoids the assumption that because research is labelled 'arts-based' this means that 'anything goes'. The inclusive view does not juxtapose arts-based with experimental methods but recognises the broad range of approaches, including more conventional qualitative research. The dance project described by Bagley and Cancienne began as a qualitative project based on the collection of interviews.

Another advantage of an inclusive view is that it is more likely to ensure a balanced perspective. As suggested earlier in this chapter it is important that objective, 'scientific' approaches do not promote a restricted vision and lose sight of the importance of context, values and human judgement in the search for universals. Research needs to work in the service of aims derived from a broader perspective of human priorities and relations rather than itself becoming master.

It is in this way that research and scholarship can avoid becoming scholarly but uninspired or scrupulous and dim-sighted as described in the introduction to this chapter. The inclusive view does not mean closing down debate; there is still room for differences of opinion about how far the scope of what counts as research should be widened. Journalism, polemic, casual speculation or anecdotal accounts of practice do not normally qualify. Instead the term 'research' in an academic context more often refers to *systematic* and *rigorous* enquiry that advances knowledge by building on what is already known. In the context of empirical work, technical aspects (such as validity, reliability and probability) become relevant because there is an expectation that research should be conducted to acceptable levels of rigour and transparency.

It is not uncommon to contrast research with other bases on which decision and judgements might be made: authority ('we do it this way because we have been told to do so'), tradition ('we have always done it this way'), prejudice ('we do it this way because no other way is acceptable') or dogma ('we do it this way because we know we are right'). This is convincing enough but there is room for difference of opinion on the relationship between research and other bases for action. Smith (2008: 190), for example, asks us to think of a poem as a piece of research: 'William Wordsworth has investigated the human condition, and these are his findings.' The question is part of an argument intended to release us from the 'debilitating assumption' that there is just 'one, hegemonic, kind of educational research' (ibid.: 192). Research, then, remains a contested concept and one over which opinions will continue to differ.

Researching the arts

In matters related to the arts there tends to be more conceptual enquiry than empirical research. This whole book therefore is arguably a discussion of research related to arts in education. However, this particular section will focus specifically on some examples of empirical research. In the last 30 years there has been considerable interest in whether involvement in the arts can lead to higher attainment in other subjects. Government agencies have been interested in this possibility, with OfSTED (1998: 3) concluding that this was a view that 'deserves serious attention'. In the USA, many arts advocates and groups have been eager to accumulate positive evidence (Deasy, 2002).

There have been several surveys of the research evidence on this question. Eisner's (1998) overview, although not one of the most recent, is still of considerable interest and relevance; it reports on the literature critically but also considers the possible negative implications of even asking whether experience in the arts boosts academic achievement. The question can suggest that the arts are inferior to other 'more academic' subjects and may conceal other questions that may be ignored in the rush for answers. What do we mean by experience of the arts? Does it relate to the number of art courses people take or has it to do with the quality of teaching? Are we referring to a long-term or a short-term benefit? He examines a range of studies in detail and highlights some of the weaknesses and challenges. For example, one study when examined suggests that the arts improve attitudes but not necessarily performance itself. It is likely that some transfer of learning is likely to occur across subjects but he points out that, 'when we talk about the effects of arts education on academic achievement in reading or mathematics we are expecting transfer of wide scope' (ibid.: 10). Eisner describes the type of research design that would be needed to go anywhere near establishing a convincing case (involving, for example randomised control and experimental groups, reliable assessment measures and consideration of the influence of teaching) but goes on to conclude:

> We do the arts no service when we try to make their case by touting their contributions to other fields. When such contributions become priorities the arts become

handmaidens to ends that are not distinctively artistic and in the process undermine the value of art's unique contributions to the education of the young.

(Ibid.: 15)

The so-called 'Mozart effect' derived from research results first published by Rauscher *et al.* (1993) that seemed to show that listening to a specific Mozart sonata might improve 'spatial-temporal reasoning'. This view received much popular attention and was extended to the claim that listening to classical music might have a beneficial effect on mental development. It also prompted further research, much of it questioning the first conclusion. A systematic overview and meta-analysis of the research evidence (Pietschnig *et al.*, 2010) examined nearly 40 studies and over 3,000 subjects and concluded that there was little support for a Mozart effect, considering the cumulative empirical evidence. There were some observed effects of exposure to the Mozart sonata (as well as any other kind of music) compared with exposure to no stimulus, but the paper suggested that this may be sufficiently explained by well-known mechanisms of 'general arousal'. This phenomenon was addressed in a paper by McBain (1961) who was interested in the 'arousal hypothesis' with regard to effect of noise on performance in the work place in the completion of monotonous tasks. He concluded that noise which is low in 'intelligibility' (or distraction value for the individual) should enhance performance in a monotonous task. His study was set in the context of wider theory dealing with the effects of environmental stimulation, generally.

There is clearly an enthusiasm to defend the arts in education against what is often constructed as a hostile social context, so the quest for evidence of the value of the arts is understandable. However, other reviews of the research have also not been convincing on this question (Harland *et al.*, 2000; Comerford *et al.*, 2005). A special edition of *Journal of Aesthetic Education* (2000) was devoted to examining the evidence of claims that arts have a positive effect on academic achievement. It contains a series of meta-analytic reviews which involved looking closely at effect sizes, evaluating the evidence from a wide range of sources. In the overview provided by the editors of that edition, they describe two overriding considerations in conducting the reviews (Winner and Hetland, 2000). The first of these was to distinguish correlation from causality. There may be evidence from a research study that students who are following arts programmes are performing better in other subjects than those who are not. However, this does not by itself show that there is a direct cause. They point out that students who choose to take art may, on average, be high academic achievers to begin with (ibid.: 5). This leads them to highlight the need for an experimental design and comparison groups to try to show causation. True experimental design is difficult – apart from practical difficulties there are ethical questions to consider in denying one group of pupils a particular educational experience that is thought to be of positive benefit. However, it also difficult to control variables, particularly in relation to quality of teaching. In some cases it may simply be that one group of teachers is better than another.

The conclusion Winner and Hetland come to is not dissimilar to some of the other overviews of research conducted in this area:

In some of the articles, we show that there is no basis for a causal connection between studying the arts and academics …. In some (but not all) areas reviewed we were able to document potentially causal relationships between studying an art form and some area of non-arts achievement.

(Ibid.: 6)

They call for more research on the issue but also warn against the academic achievement argument, insisting that 'the presence of the arts in our schools should not rest on whether or not learning in the arts transfers to other academic domains' (ibid.: 7).

Empirical research in the arts is not confined to examining the relationship between art education and academic achievement. The study by Harland *et al.* (2000: 504) in the UK sought to investigate the range of outcomes attributed to arts education and analyse the key factors and processes that might bring about those effects. They used case studies of five secondary schools, questionnaires, interviews and wider sources of information related to examination performance. There were a number of interesting findings from this study but one in particular was the perception from students that the different art forms generated distinctive effects. Dance offered increased awareness of the body and movement, art promoted expressive skills, drama nurtured empathy and the valuing of others and music extended active listening skills (ibid.: 566). We might note in passing that some of these effects are somewhat limited but the identification of the *different* effects is important and will be addressed further in Chapter 8.

Chapter 2 of this book began with an account of how 13-year-old students classified a number of activities as 'art' or 'not art'. This data was from a pilot project that sought to examine students' views on a variety of questions related to the arts. The original intention was that the larger-scale project would then relate student responses to a number of variables, particularly age, to examine how concepts of art developed and matured. There might also be the potential for cross-cultural comparisons. For that purpose the responses needed to convert easily into statistics, hence the closed questions in the pilot, with the possibility of the pupils providing additional comments either on paper or in follow-up interviews. As often happens, the responses from the pilot project led to a rather different line of thinking. The challenge was to devise practical tasks which could be used as an initial attempt to elicit children's constructs and might function as a stimulus to further discussion. A summary of a small number of the tasks and the percentage responses follows.

The students were presented with a picture of a bridge that had been wrapped by the artist Christo and asked to tick the statement which best represented their responses. The replies are given in Table 4.1.

In another task they were shown a print of Picasso's *Weeping Woman* and a very representational photograph of a woman weeping and asked to say which they preferred, the

TABLE 4.1 Responses to a picture of a wrapped bridge

RESPONSE	NO.
This is a total waste of time and money	26
I like this because it looks good	40
This looks interesting but I am not sure why	14
I like this because it makes me think	26

Picasso (71 per cent) or the photograph (28 per cent). Similarly, when asked to choose between a Henry Moore sculpture (57 per cent) and a statue of a man with a ladder (47 per cent), numbers divided fairly evenly. The number of students who revealed preferences for more abstract and challenging works was larger than expected. What became more interesting, however, was not the statistical responses but some of the students' incidental comments and the way they engaged in the task. Some of the comments reported in Chapter 2 (e.g. 'It doesn't really make you think', 'art is something you learn to do') revealed embryonic theories of art. When asked to divide a series of activities as listed in Table 4.2 into two groups and provide reasons, their comments revealed perceptions related to class as well as the elements of inclusive and separatist views of art: 'classy enter-tainment (play, orchestra, cricket, ballet) and common (others)'; 'things rehearsed and luck or chance'; 'day to day activities'; 'one group is more casual and one is more posh'; 'more sophisticated artistic things that posh people watch are in A and B is normal people'.

Some of the students' responses were reminiscent of some earlier research on con-structs of poetry (Fleming, 1992). Here the pupils were asked to say whether a series of short texts were poetry or not poetry and give reasons. The pupils employed a range of criteria in making judgements about texts. Poetry was seen by some as heightened or marked use of language ('Poets use different or better words to describe their subjects'). Others emphasised the notion of managed construction ('it is laid out with thought and pattern'). One or two even alluded to the power of the reader in creating meaning: 'I like poetry because it gives you a different view point and you interpret what is happening your own way. If you read a piece of poetry through the second time you read it carefully, it means something else altogether'.

It was clear from both research projects that 13-year-old pupils were able to begin to engage with conceptual questions about the nature of art and poetry itself. This raises question about the place of meta-cognition in the teaching of art, the degree to which students' appreciation of art might be enhanced by questions and discussions of a more philosophical nature (appropriately adapted for the age group) on, for example, the role of intention, the nature of art, the high art / low art distinction, notions of plurality of meaning, and the place of art in different societies.

TABLE 4.2 Dividing activities task

Here is a list of activities the people do:
Watching television Watching football match Watching a play Listening to an orchestra at a music concert Watching a live pop group Watching a film Watching a cricket match Watching a ballet (a) Divide the activities into two groups by writing the letter A or B beside each item. Please note there is no 'correct' answer – there may be different ways of dividing them. You do not have to have the same number of activities in each group. (b) Please give a reason why you have divided the activities in that way.

Further reading

The International Handbook of Research in Arts Education in two volumes (Bresler, 2007) contains a large number of papers by different authors with sections on history, curriculum, assessment and evaluation, composition, appreciation, museums and cultural centres, informal learning, child culture, social and cultural issues, the body, creativity, technology and spirituality. *The Handbook of Research and Policy in Art Education* (Eisner and Day, 2004) is more specifically related to visual art with many of the papers of wider relevance. It has sections, each containing several chapters, on historical currents in art education, policy perspectives impacting on the teaching of art, learning in the visual arts, teaching and teacher education, forms of assessment in art education and emerging visions of the field. (For arts-based research see Cahnmann-Taylor and Siegesmund, 2008; Liamputtong and Rumbold, 2008; Barone and Eisner, 2011.) Research papers can be found in *Journal of Aesthetic Education* and *International Journal of Education and the Arts*. There also journals for each of the art subjects. For papers on the arts more generally see *The British Journal of Aesthetics*. Leavy (2009) addresses arts-based research in *Method Meets Art*. See also a review by Ward and Bagley (2010).

5

Historical perspectives

Introduction

In Muriel Spark's (1961: 11) novel *The Prime of Miss Jean Brodie*, Miss Brodie is telling her class of young girls about her summer holiday: 'I must tell you about the Italian paintings I saw. Who is the greatest Italian painter?' Back comes the reply, 'Leonardo da Vinci, Miss Brodie'. 'That is incorrect. The answer is Giotto, he is my favourite.' The satirical intent is clear in the self-centredness and certainty of the answer, although, on reflection the question as to how a teacher strikes a balance between appropriate guidance and indoctrination is not easy. There is another interesting issue here, however, to do with whether it is entirely appropriate to compare two painters born nearly 200 years apart who had a significant but different impact on the history of painting. To what degree should judgement be based purely on response to their work or to what degree should historical and contextual issues also be considered?

This chapter will examine ways in which a historical perspective may help illuminate understanding of arts in education. Three broad possibilities come to mind: an exploration of the history of art itself, history of ideas about art, and history of arts in education. These areas are closely related. It is difficult to distinguish the development of art from the development of *ideas* about art, particularly if implicit rather than just explicit theories are taken into account, for as Osborne (1968: 20) has said, 'The theory of art which dominates any period of history can seldom be found fully articulate in that period'. The history of arts in education is more distinct as it was less directly influenced by art theory and more by psychology and more general social and political pressures. The challenge of providing a perspective drawn from history is compounded by the fact that thinking about history itself has evolved. We are reminded in Jenkins' *Re-thinking History* (2003: xi) that history is not the same as the past and that even bothering to point that out now seems 'quaintly old fashioned'. As with language itself, the narratives formulated about the past are not innocent and do not constitute a transparent window on past reality, 'The histories we assign to things and people are composed, created, constituted, constructed and always situated literatures' (ibid.: xi). In other words the analytic account that a particular history provides in the way it selects, categorises, and divides the world should not be taken for granted. For example, a history of England conceived narrowly as a history of kings and queens has obvious limitations. As Evans (2011: 11) has pointed out, such an approach can lead to a narrow celebratory history aimed primarily at cementing national identity and excluding consideration of wider social developments.

The discipline of art history has also undergone fundamental change in recent decades (Harris, 2001: 1). The influence of perspectives drawn from critical theory, Marxism, post-colonialism and feminism has challenged established ideas. The more radical view that emerged from much of the theorising in the 1960s is illustrated by Berger's 1971 television series and book *Ways of Seeing* (1972). Here he challenges the traditional account of Gainsborough's painting of Mr and Mrs Andrews as being a work that reflects an idyllic country scene, a manifestation of the author's 'Rousseauism' (Clark, 1961) by giving it a rather different slant: 'They are not a couple in Nature as Rousseau imagined nature. They are landowners and their proprietary attitude towards what surrounds them is visible in their stance and their expressions' (Berger, 1972: 107).

Berger goes on to remind us of some of the contextual details surrounding the owning of estates: the sentence for poaching at that time was deportation, and if a man stole a potato he risked a public whipping. The growth of feminism in the 1970s is also reflected in Berger's interpretation of well-known paintings of nudes in which the image of the woman is designed to flatter the male spectator (ibid.: 64). Some of these interpretations may now seem a little narrow but they served to broaden awareness and question assumptions that were previously taken for granted. After all, as commentators started to realise, there are no women artists identified in Gombrich's (1995) history of art (Harris, 2001: 37; Nochlin, 1971). They also help to liberate us from the assumption that the meaning of a work is determined by the conscious intention of the artist. Contemporary approaches to art history, then, are more inclined to recognise its plurality, making it more accurate to refer to 'art histories' rather than a singular tradition (Pooke and Newall, 2008). Harris (2001: 2) characterises the new art history as being more 'open, interrogative (questioning) and self-critical than ever before'. In this approach, art is seen more in relation to its social history, based on a belief that 'artworks, artists, and art history should be understood as artefacts, agents, structures and practices rooted materially in social life and meaningful only within those circumstances of production and interpretation' (ibid.: 264). This way of thinking is part of a more inclusive than separatist perspective and has implications for teaching, in that in addition to form and content, the consideration of social context when studying works of art may open up new possibilities of understanding. This is a very different conception from the traditional habit of providing anodyne background details on the artist's life, but rather includes a consideration of ideological context to challenge thinking.

Art history does not have to be taught in a boring way. Kok (2011) describes a project in which a group of young people transformed their learning about Islamic calligraphy into the development of their own art product. They had learned that Islamic calligraphy is found in architecture, painting and pottery, and used this knowledge to create their own vase. After extensive experimentation and design activities they used wire to craft the vase, whose design reflected the calligraphy they had studied. The project combined objectives related to art history, intercultural learning and design. It also stimulated thought about the nature of art in other cultures when they understood the important religious context and saw that handwriting itself is often seen as an art form.

That our conventional ways of thinking may be more arbitrary than we realise is illustrated graphically by Foucault (1989). In his preface to *The Order of Things* he describes the way animals are listed in a Chinese encyclopaedia in such categories as (a) belonging to the emperor, (b) embalmed, (c) tame, (d) suckling pigs, etc. This list was a source of amusement to him but also of 'wonderment' and insight, for the effect of the 'exotic charm of another system of thought' was to expose the potential limitation of our own, 'the stark impossibility of thinking *that*' (ibid.: xvi). This is in effect a recognition of the importance of being able to decentre, to see things from a different perspective as well as a recognition of the way in which particular systems of thought may constrain rather than expand thinking. Later on in the same book Foucault provides a very detailed analysis of a painting by Velázquez (*Las Meninas*) showing the artist himself taking a moment's pause from working on a canvas to look out at us, the place occupied by the viewer of the painting. For Foucault, the composition of the painting is a very early challenge to the notion that reality can be simply 'represented'; representation is not simply a 'window on the world', a means of capturing an external order as was often thought. There are parallels, then, with representation in art, the way history represents the world and indeed in the relation of language to reality.

Ideas and definitions of art are not timeless nor are they outside history, but relate to the assumptions of the societies which forge them (Pooke and Newall, 2008: 8). Just as art can expand our vision and help us to see things differently, history can do the same as long as we are alert to the fact that it can also limit perception if we are too ready to accept over-simplified generalisations. At any one time we only tend to perceive that which particular contemporary conventions determine what we see. Similarly the language (or discourse) in which ideas are expressed may impose limitations on understanding.

Continuity and change

This section will not attempt a detailed history but will instead focus on some of the changing ideas about art that have potential to illuminate issues related to arts in education. We have already seen in Chapter 3 how much thinking in arts education was dominated by popular conceptions derived from romanticism. That does not make them entirely wrong but it can alert us to a potential limitation of vision in that the creation of art was prioritised over response to art works. There are other topics relevant to education that also benefit from a historical perspective: the distinction between art and craft, the relationship between art and morality and the emphasis on individuality.

It is fairly commonplace to read that the Greeks did not have a concept of 'art' or the 'aesthetic'. This statement is both accurate and potentially misleading, both true and not true. It is true in that, in Foucault's terms, concepts are not static, and change through different periods of thinking. Likewise Levinson (1993: 411) has recognised that virtually all concepts are subject to historical evolution. In classical Greek there was no word that easily translates into the modern concept of 'art'. That does not necessarily mean that our concept of art would have been entirely alien to the classical mind. Plato specifically addressed the role of the arts in education in the *Republic* Books 2 and 3, while much of Artistotle's *Poetics* can be read as a challenge to Plato's criticism of poetry (Pappas, 2001: 15). As pointed out in Chapter 2, the Greek word *techne*, which is often translated as 'art', denoted a skill or craft. However, it was thought of not merely as manual skill rather 'as a branch of knowledge, a form of practical science' (Osborne, 1968: 17). Although there was no concept of fine art in the way we understand that term, there was an implicit concept of the aesthetic in that artefacts were embellished with ornamentation *beyond* their practical utility. This integration of the utilitarian and aesthetic is a reminder that the emphasis on fine art with its focus on pure aesthetic appeal is relatively recent. The separation of art and craft that would have made little sense in the classical world can also be seen as part of a broader picture that has downgraded practical skills and practical intelligence in contemporary educational thinking in favour of narrow cognitive ability. Victoria Coren (2011) writing in *The Observer* points out that 'Some children's brains come alive for practical or visual skills, some for flights of mental fancy; you don't need to define them as more or less "clever"'. She continues,

> I had a plumber round here the other day, talking about his disappointing son. 'He's a bit slow,' the plumber revealed. 'He could never make it in plumbing. I once left him to drill six holes in a wall. Came back an hour later, he hadn't even managed one of them. Poor lad he isn't the smartest.' 'What does he do now?' I asked. 'He works for the civil service', said the plumber, sadly. It was a salutary lesson in perspective.

An emphasis on historical continuity rather than on differences in ideas about art lends itself more to a naturalistic view which sees art as a universal and persistent need in human existence. It is thus seen as central to human nature. It is customary to point to the presence of some form of art in every culture throughout history to support that view. However, there is no consensus about the meaning and interpretation of such early works as the Palaeolithic cave paintings found in Lascaux and elsewhere. Hauser (1962: 5) suggests that to see them purely as decorative is untenable because the paintings were often found in inaccessible places with no sign of habitation. Some ascribe to them a religious or ceremonial purpose possibly derived from hallucinations (Spivey, 2005). They are in the main pictures of animals, prompting the view that the act of representation was a magical effort to control (Hauser, 1962). Werner Herzog's documentary film *Cave of Forgotten Dreams* about the older Palaeolithic works discovered in France in 1994, brings the paintings to life vividly but is rightly inconclusive about their original function. It is tempting to impose an interpretation that fits one's preferred conception of art but it is not necessary to have a full understanding of purpose and meaning to recognise in these and similar works both a broad universal artistic drive and a potential challenge to restricted notions of how art should function in society.

In addition to examining history, perspectives may also be broadened by considering art from other cultures with an open mind. Osborne (1968: 82) points out that at a time when a western view saw art as some part of reality (actual or ideal, observed or imagined), Chinese art theory saw this feature as relatively unimportant: 'Attention is concentrated on the art work as a reality in its own right, which by its technical and structural rhythms bodies forth and makes manifest the unifying cosmic principle of the Tao.' Shiner (2008) warns against the view the concept of art has an essential, universal core. On this basis, objects from small-scale traditional societies in non-Western cultures may be interpreted purely in terms of a modern understanding of the concept of 'art'.

He argues that 're-classifying and appropriating ritual objects and performances as "art" was at best a form of positive ethnocentrism, at worst a form of cultural imperialism' (ibid.: 264). To take a sacred object from one culture and display it as 'art' in another may be to distort and diminish it. He also recognises a danger of circularity in arguments about the universality of 'art'. If we adopt a sufficiently broad concept of art then the argument that all these objects are art is fairly easy to sustain. However, it is wrong to claim that the separatist concept of fine art, a much narrower notion, is universal. From an educational perspective the interest lies in further arguments in favour of broadening what can now be seen as a fairly recent and Western concept of the autonomy of art and the aesthetic.

The autonomy of art does not appear to have been part of the medieval mind where according to Margolis (2001: 27) there was an 'overriding concern with the conceptual relationship between Creator and Creation'. Art frequently served a didactic purpose of instructing an illiterate population in the faith. The link between art and morality persisted throughout history but increasingly in less direct and more subtle ways. A less didactic association of art with morality has been addressed by contemporary writers (Hamilton, 2003; Nusbaum, 1990; Palmer, 1992). The alternative to seeing the relationship between art and morality in terms of a very narrow notion of rules takes two broad forms. One is to assert the very broadest relationship described in Chapter 1 in the sense of revealing humanity or showing the fullness of life. However, there is also a role played by art in showing us the subtle gradations of moral judgements. This is particularly the case with the novel and is exemplified perfectly in Jane Austen where the initially more attractive characters such as the Crawfords in *Mansfield Park* are revealed not as being evil but morally lacking in some way. As so much narrative fiction and drama reveals, judging human quality is rarely a black-and-white matter. What appears to be generosity may be better described as self-aggrandisement. In a teaching relationship, kindness and support may become indulgence. When does respect become sycophancy? When does modesty become false modesty? The development of moral virtue is more complex than is often assumed and we can turn to art, and fiction in particular, to have our moral discernment and sensibility sharpened.

A frequently recognised aspect of the transition from the Middle Ages to the Renaissance is the perception of the latter period as the era of the rise of the individual. In 1860 Burckhardt had published *The Civilization of the Renaissance in Italy* in which he took the view that in the Middle Ages, 'man was conscious of himself only as a member of a race, people, party, family, or corporation – only through some general category' (Burckhardt, 1929: 129). The Christian conception found in Paul (Rom. 12.4–8; 1 Cor. 12) of 'the body of Christ as a charismatic community' can be seen as 'imagery drawn from the political philosophy of the time' (Dunn, 2008: 1). The emphasis on community had a practical as well as philosophical/religious basis. The development of guilds during the later Middle Ages was significant in that the only power and influence artists had during this period was based more on their collective rather than individual identity. As Ward (2010: 35) has pointed out, the individual medieval artist was often not identified with the work; the Wilton Diptych, for example, painted for Richard II, was anonymous. It became widely accepted amongst cultural commentators that a key feature of the Renaissance was the awakening of the self and the development of the individual

(Garner, 1990: 49). Similar themes are found in MacMurray (1933), Van den Berg (1961), Williams (1961) and more recently Foucault (see Logan, 1986). The Middle Ages, in contrast, did not value originality and spontaneity as much, but instead recommended the imitation of the masters and thought plagiarism permissible (Hauser, 1962: 61). Moreover, it is the Renaissance that is associated with the recognition of genius and the idea that the work of art is the creation of an autocratic personality (ibid.: 61). All of these considerations can be associated with a move from a communal to a more individual emphasis, although not all commentators accept that it appropriate to attribute the 'rise of the individual' to the Renaissance.

Martin (1997: 1311) is one of the writers who has questioned whether it appropriate to approach the Renaissance in traditional Burckhardtian terms. His argument is not dissimilar to the warnings about the dangers of applying a contemporary concept of art to earlier periods. For both arguments rely on an assumption that there are universal concepts that persist. He makes the following observation:

> Recent philosophical, anthropological, and literary models of the individual have so transformed our understanding of the human person that it is no longer possible to base our analysis of the origins of individualism on the traditional humanistic assumptions that Burckhardt took as a given.
>
> (Ibid.: 1311)

There are two issues of particular interest here. One is further confirmation of the general difficulty of applying concepts across eras and a warning about the folly of making generalisations too readily – a theme that has emerged several times already in this book. The other is more directly related to education. Despite the considerable amount of theory that emphasises the social aspects of learning (Vygostky, 1962) there is still a predominant emphasis on the individual in our education system. As seen in Chapter 1, justification of art is often formulated in terms of individual benefits. The medieval perspective (also found in other cultures) that places more emphasis on a communal concept is at least a challenge to accepted norms. Similarly, the medieval perspective may at least call into question the excessive focus on the importance of originality and the fear of plagiarism in arts education that emerged from the emphasis on self-expression.

Arts education

Any historical account runs the risk of either focusing on detail to such a degree that there is no recognition of broad patterns, or of identifying distinct patterns but in doing so distorting the truth. Despite those dangers, a historical perspective on the development of arts education in a specific context is valuable not only because many contemporary issues have their origins in the past but also because many of the issues and tensions still persist. In particular, issues related to the justification of the arts and ideas about what counts as art can be further illuminated in this way. The account in this section draws on Fleming's (2010) *Art in Education and Creativity* but focuses more on the approaches to arts education in the pre- and post-Second World War periods. It is also concerned more with the way the arts were addressed in government policy documents rather than more general publications, although there was often an association between the two because they sometimes had committee members or authors in common (for example Nunn, 1920; Holmes, 1911).

At the time when compulsory schooling was introduced through the 1870 Elementary Education Act, the arts were largely ignored in official publications. This is in some ways understandable because the struggle was to establish basic education, find sufficient numbers of teachers, and address the considerable health problems that existed amongst the young. The contents page of the 1870 Act had such headings as 'supply of schools, constitution of school board, expenses, accounts and audit, attendance at school' with little reference to curriculum or subjects. These were largely taken for granted with the emphasis largely on rote learning and drilling in basic skills. The earlier revised code of 1862 that had introduced payment by results stipulated that every scholar for whom grants were claimed must be examined according to one of six 'standards' in reading, writing and arithmetic. The strongly utilitarian attitude reinforced the conception of the arts as a peripheral luxury or leisure activity rather than as a basic need. The term 'arts in education' was rarely used in official publications but instead terms such as 'crafts', 'fine art' or 'aesthetic training' appear.

A series of reports published in subsequent years give more insight into ideas about curriculum and arts provision than the education Acts. The first chapter of the Hadow report of 1923 on the *Differentiation of the Curriculum for Boys and Girls Respectively in Secondary Schools* begins with a history of the recent curriculum in private boys and girls schools and thus gives a useful insight into the nineteenth-century priorities (Board of Education, 1923). In the period up to about 1860 the prevailing tradition of girls' education was that it should be completely different from that of boys, and should consist mainly of 'accomplishments' that is to say, 'a slight proficiency in Music, Languages and Literature, Drawing, Painting and Needlework' (ibid.: 2). Boys, on the other hand, studied the classics, 'with some smattering of divinity, geography and history, often taught through the medium of Latin' (ibid.: 6). One school was singled out for mention as being of considerable interest 'on account of its recognition of the importance of the teaching of English and of aesthetic subjects, especially Music and Art' (ibid.: 12).

Members of the committee who interviewed witnesses to gather evidence to write the report were impressed by the 'almost unanimous agreement' on the 'desirability of developing the aesthetic side of secondary education' (Board of Education, 1923: 60). The report commented on 'the relative neglect of Music, Drawing and Painting, and other forms of aesthetic training' which was 'less noticeable in girls' schools, which inherit from the older tradition of women's education a sense of the importance of the fine Arts' (ibid.: 60). The report however is a little vague on both the definition of, and the value, of the fine arts, suggesting that they develop 'concentration of mind, accuracy of observation, and a genuine appreciation of natural beauty and artistic achievement' and stimulate 'the growth of the imaginative, critical, and creative faculties' (ibid.: 67). The report placed some value on the importance of developing the power of appreciating the fine arts but almost as a second best alternative, 'as there is ample evidence to show that many pupils are able to enjoy them who have little technical skill in any of the aesthetic media' (ibid.: 70).

The 1931 Hadow report on primary education (Board of Education, 1931) struck a more visionary note, reflecting some of the progressive thinking that had been slowly gaining ground amongst earlier writers (Edgeworth and Edgeworth, 1855; Holmes, 1911; Nunn, 1920). The general aim of education 'should be to develop in the child the fundamental human powers and to awaken him to the fundamental interests of civilised life' (Board of Education, 1931: 93). The report recognised the importance of a developmental perspective on the growth of the child, illustrating the greater attention to psychology than philosophy, which might have brought more conceptual clarity. It also recognised the particular needs of younger pupils rather than seeing the primary school purely as a preparation for secondary education. It placed emphasis on thinking rather than rote learning and on the pupils being active rather than passive, and suggested that 'a good school, in short, is not a place of compulsory instruction, but a community of old and young, engaged in learning by co-operative experiment' (Board of Education, 1931: xv). The report has a section on the aesthetic development of children (ibid.: 44) between the ages of seven and eleven but there is no coherent account of the role of the arts. There is a recognition that 'owing to the bookish trend of modern instruction, mental images, so concrete and so vivid in the younger child, tend to atrophy from disuse' but no further discussion of how a concept of the aesthetic may related to learning (ibid.: 45). It suggests that artistic ability and appreciation in the young depend upon the level of intelligence (though they are less closely correlated with it than any other subject of the school curriculum) and special aptitudes or talents. However, there is little discussion of the implications of this view for teaching or the curriculum.

The section on 'aesthetic subjects' is well meaning but distinctly vague. Handwork and drawing are seen as 'useful as ancillary means of learning about other things' but 'they should also hold an important place in their own right' (ibid.: 97). The only time the word 'art' appears in this section is when it is applied to handwriting, which should be taught 'as a mode of art as well as a useful instrument' (ibid.: 99). In painting, music and verse, pupils need to be encouraged 'by a teacher who knows how to direct without interfering with their unsophisticated sincerity' (ibid.: 97). The section finishes with the rather inconclusive statement 'Of music we need say nothing here except to indicate that we count it among the indispensable elements of the primary school curriculum' (ibid.: 99), although both music and drama get more attention in the next section in a discussion of physical training.

The Spens report (Board of Education, 1938: 171) wanted a 'more prominent place' for 'aesthetic subjects'. It contains separate chapters on scripture and on English, classics, mathematics and general science, but none specifically devoted to the arts. It recommended that the curriculum should include 'some forms of art, including Music, the most universal of the arts' and that 'handicrafts, should be taught with emphasis either on the aesthetic aspect, as in weaving, carving, handwriting, or on the constructional aspect, as in carpentry and needlecraft' (ibid.: 157). The Norwood report (Secondary School Examination Council, 1943), perhaps taking a lead from the structure of Holmes' *What Is and What Might Be*, has two chapters devoted to 'secondary education as it is' and 'secondary education as it might be'. It concluded that secondary schools had been asked to do too much, and recommended three types of education, thought of as the secondary Grammar, the secondary Technical, the secondary Modern. It took the view that arts subjects should not be seen as 'extras' nor regarded as 'an offset or relief to other subjects' and that 'they have not received the attention in schools which is due to them'

(Secondary School Examination Council, 1943: 122). However, once again, there is little clarity or little indication of how these goals might be realised.

Although there was innovative work in the arts in the pre-war period from individuals such as Harriet Finlay-Johnson (1911), Henry Caldwell Cook (1917) and Marion Richardson (1948), their influence was limited and it was the government reports and education acts that had more potential to affect practice. The impression from these reports is one of earnest but muddled thinking. There is little evidence of coherent thinking about the nature and purpose of the arts but instead a switch between concepts of art, craft and aesthetic training. Dancing, singing and drawing were encouraged in different contexts but these tended to be recognised more as crafts and were not treated as a composite group. When they are not seen as leisure time activities, the value of the arts subjects was often seen in relation to their practical value and their contribution to skills development.

The post-war period was characterised by the steady development of progressive ideas which inevitably influenced the approach to the arts. As described in Chapter 1, Abb's (1987) analysis in terms of changing paradigms is a useful way of understanding developments in this period. The progressive, child-centred approach placed emphasis on the values of self-expression in the creation of art particularly in dance, drama and visual art. The more inclusive approach embraced responding and appreciation as well as making and the importance of tradition. This clear-cut division between paradigms was less evident in government reports. The 1959 handbook published by the Ministry of Education focused on primary education and extolled the virtues of 'the native power of imaginative expression' in its section on art, craft and needlework (Board of Education, 1959: 213); these terms are used in preference to the concept of the aesthetic. The Crowther report's declaration that pupils 'are not flowers, but roots of education' (Central Advisory Council for England, 1959: 218) was fairly typical in that this warm but rather general endorsement was not matched by very much detailed discussion.

The key government report in the post-war period came in 1967 from the Central Advisory Council for Education, the Plowden Report. This report was not focused on the arts nor even exclusively on the curriculum. Later criticisms often failed to recognise its achievements, particularly the establishment of education priority areas which derived from the acknowledgement in the report of the way on which social background was a key influence on educational success. The report also recognised the need to expand nursery provision and the importance of participation by parents. Where the report was vulnerable was in its conception of the relationship between teaching and learning and came under fire from philosophers (Peters, 1969). Some of the criticisms are summarised in Wilkinson (1987), Gillard (2004) and Pollard (1987).

The type of enthusiasm for the arts found in previous reports also appears in Plowden. Visual art is 'both a form of communication and a means of expression of feelings which ought to permeate the whole curriculum and the whole life of the school. A society which neglects or despises it is dangerously sick' (Central Advisory Council for Education, 1967: 247). The section on music has little on aims but is more concerned with practicalities to do with teacher training. The report saw a place for drama primarily within English. Dance is acknowledged and promoted within the section on physical education.

Abbs' account of two paradigms is also a useful way of getting a broad focus on more contemporary developments in art education. The movement from an obsession with individual self-expression to a more inclusive view that also embraced 'responding' and 'evaluating' as well as 'making' is reflected in the developments in the National Curriculum. The publication of *All Our Futures* (NACCCE, 1999) gave rise to a number of initiatives and partnerships, although it did not impact on the National Curriculum as the authors had hoped. The burgeoning interest in creativity and in particular creativity across the curriculum has been significant in more recent years.

As well as the challenge to thinking on specific issues such as individualism one of the key lessons from history is the danger of imposing narrow interpretations on events and forming too many pre-conceptions. It would be ironic if the conclusion to this chapter fell into that trap. However, in many of the government reports there is a lack of understanding and a lack of conceptual discrimination which might have been achieved by drawing on some of the contemporary writing on art theory. There is a degree of confusion as to whether the arts should be taught for their own sake or as a form of skills training or physical exercise. The uncertainty about whether arts should be seen in their own right or primarily as a form of creative learning persists. This distinction between 'learning in' and 'learning through' is the subject of the next chapter.

Further reading

Beardlsey, M. (1966) *Aesthetics: From Classical Greece to the Present* is still a useful overview. For a contemporary approach to (visual) art history see Elkins (2002) *Stories of Art*. *The Blackwell Guide to Aesthetics* (Kivy, 2004) has relevant chapters by Guyer, 'The Origins of Modern Aesthetics 1711–35', and by Carroll, 'Art and The Moral Realm'. For a discussion of the concept of human nature see Midgley (1995) *Beast and Man* and Pinker (2002) *The Blank Slate*; the latter has a provocative chapter on 'The Arts'. For a series of chapters by different authors on art and moral issues, including one on 'Art and Moral Education' see Bermúdez and Gardner (2003) *Art and Morality*. Sennett's (2008) *The Craftsman* considers craftsmanship in a broad context with a strong historical angle. The website *The History of Education in England* maintained by Derek Gillard is an excellent resource containing most of the major UK government documents and reports, Acts of Parliament and other relevant documents and articles (www.educationengland.org.uk/index.html).

6

Learning in and learning through the arts

Introduction

Amongst the various themes that have emerged in this book, two are particularly relevant to this chapter: inclusive/separatist conceptions of art and extrinsic/intrinsic justifications. In a chapter published in *The Routledge International Handbook of Creative Learning* I made the case that these dichotomies can be associated with concepts of *learning in* and *learning through* the arts, and that this connection provides a valuable link between theory and practice (Fleming, 2011b). At its simplest, *learning through*, as the preposition suggests, looks beyond the art form itself to outcomes that are extrinsic, and often takes place when the arts are employed across the curriculum to further learning in other subjects, e.g. the use of visual art to teach reading, the use of drama to teach history, the use of dance to teach religious education. *Learning in* the arts more often refers to learning within the subject or discipline itself, learning that pertains to the particular art form. However, the distinction is not just a matter of curriculum organisation but may also extend to how aims are defined within the art subject itself.

This chapter will examine whether the concepts of *learning in* and *learning through* stand up to scrutiny as distinct approaches to justifying and teaching the arts, and whether they provide a helpful focus for maintaining a balanced approach to evaluating practice. It will be suggested that the distinction between *learning in* and *learning through* is easy to maintain when more obvious examples are considered. However, it is when the concepts become less distinct and start to merge that the greater interest and insight is found.

Learning through

The concept of *learning in* is more elusive than *learning through* but even the latter concept is not as straightforward as is sometimes thought, particularly when it is applied to art subjects themselves and not only in a cross-curricular context. With regard to *learning through*, confusion may be caused if no distinction is made between intentional aims, on the one hand, and contingent benefits or outcomes that are more incidental, on the other (this was addressed briefly in Chapter 1). It is one thing to argue that the engagement with the arts may bring all sorts of extra advantages (a 'soft' formulation of *learning through*) but it is rather a different matter to suggest that the aims should be conceived primarily in those terms or that the organisation of the curriculum and the teaching of the subject should be determined on the basis of such benefits (a 'hard' formulation of *learning through*). For example, a soft version of *learning through* may recognise that engagement with the arts can increase confidence, appreciate the environment or improve cognitive ability without this affecting the way the subject is taught. On the other hand, a hard version of *learning through* might influence the actual teaching of the art subject with more emphasis on 'making' rather than 'responding', or might even result in abandoning its separate teaching completely, conceiving it instead as a pedagogic method to teach other subjects.

These different approaches are clearly exemplified in the case of drama. As reflected in the titles of some key publications, drama teaching was conceived by many writers in terms of *learning through* both as a subject in itself and across the curriculum: *Development Through Drama* (Way, 1967), *Learning Through Drama* (McGregor *et al.*, 1977), *Drama as Education* (Bolton, 1984), *Learning Through Imagined Experience* (Neelands, 1992), *The Drama of History* (Fines and Verrier, 1974), *Drama For Learning* (Heathcote and Bolton, 1994). After the introduction of the National Curriculum in England and Wales in 1987, drama was not officially identified as a separate subject; it found a place primarily within English but was also referenced in other subjects. The then National Curriculum Council produced a poster summarising the references to drama in English, science, technology, history and modern foreign languages (NCC, 1990). Even so, many advocates objected to the failure to recognise drama as a separate subject (Davis and Byron, 1988; Goode, 1988) This was attributed by Hornbrook to the widespread growth of a *learning through* approach, advocates of which were seen as 'unwitting collaborators' in the marginalisation of drama:

> A high-priesthood of practitioners has succeeded in isolating school drama from the mainstream of dramatic theory and practice by defining it, not as the study of theatres, actors and plays but as a specialised kind of internalised process – a 'learning medium' with miraculous pedagogic powers.
>
> (Hornbrook, 1992: 18)

The phrase 'drama as a learning medium' was widely used, and the drama education world became divided between advocates of drama as opposed to theatre, and process as opposed to product (Way, 1967; Hornbrook, 1989). *Learning through* and *learning in* were associated with these different positions in some cases with misleading consequences.

A key criticism of the approach to drama that focused on its extrinsic benefits was that it had lost sight of the art form. When art is harnessed in the service of other curriculum subjects there is a danger that the objectives of the non-art subject become dominant at the expense of artistic form and quality. More emphasis tends to placed on the *experience* of the learner rather more than the *art product* itself (Dewey, 2005). The learning outcomes are more likely to be of an 'ancillary' nature rather than arts based (Eisner, 1998). However, a closer scrutiny of actual practice reveals that this is a possible but not a necessary consequence of *learning through*. For example, one approach to the use of drama to explore the discovery of the Sutton Hoo treasure in history might be to put the pupils into groups to make up a play on the subject, using a form of *learning through* drama. Unless the class are extremely experienced in drama it is likely that their work will largely involve superficial playing without any dramatic form. Artistic integrity is sacrificed to subject learning. However, this is only one possible approach.

An alternative approach might invite pupils to act out the parts of specialist historians and archaeologists (Fleming, 2011a: 32). They imagine that the Sutton Hoo discovery was recently made and they are to offer a second opinion to corroborate the findings of an 'expert' (the teacher in role) who is about to publish a book on the breakthrough. Pupils in the course of their dramatic enactment examine photographs, take measurements, reconstruct the scene of the discovery and re-enact scenes of what might have happened at the time. They temporarily withhold the actual knowledge they have in order for their scientific work to proceed and 'discoveries' to be made in the course of the drama. They address a number of questions pertaining to the find: Why was the treasure still there when so many barrows had been robbed by earlier treasure hunters? Why was a body never found? Why was treasure buried when someone died? What sort of value did the treasure have to them – was it seen as art and, if so, what did this mean? The author of the book (teacher in role) seeks to persuade the experts to agree with his mistaken interpretations (he did not even recognise that this was the tomb of a king) and then to collude with him in repressing the truth. The pupils find themselves defending and articulating the intrinsic importance of establishing historical truth, having explored ways in which the past is reconstructed. In the course of the drama they also examine the way historical interpretations depend on selection of sources and distinguish between fact and point of view. The difference between this example and the preceding one is that it is the elements of the art form such as focus, tension, suspension of disbelief that feed into the meaningful learning. Arguably, this is as much a case of *learning in* as it is of *learning through*. Notice also that the approach which asks pupils to get into groups to make a play about Sutton Hoo not only does not make full use of art form but is not likely to achieve any depth of learning, at best only serving to reinforce what the pupils know.

A similar ambiguity can be found in examples from other arts subjects. Richards (2003) addresses the use of visual art to teach reading, and this seems at first glance to be a clear case of *learning through*. The details, however, show that this designation is not entirely justified. The case described is one in which an art specialist worked in partnership with a class teacher to *combine* objectives related to both the arts and reading: 'Throughout the year, students explore the arts of great artists and cultures of the world. They develop an understanding and an appreciation for art and classical music that spill over into a passion for reading literature' (ibid.: 20). The author suggests that that the experiences of studying lines, shapes, colours, unity and space in art 'heighten print awareness and facilitate the comprehension of words and the development of other reading skills' (ibid.: 21). In other words, *learning in* the art form does not get excluded by the more extrinsic objectives. It may therefore be helpful to distinguish between (1) using the arts as a contingent method for teaching other subjects and (2) including the arts as a component subject in an integrated approach to planning and teaching the curriculum. A more integrated approach in which the concepts of *learning in* and *learning through* are not so easily distinguished will pay due attention to the learning outcomes of both subjects, seeking to blend them.

Abbs (2003) takes the view that *learning through* dominated arts education through much of the twentieth century largely in the form of 'personal growth' aims. As discussed in Chapter 3 the influence of progressive, child-centred approaches emerged in the early twentieth century in part as a challenge to the earlier authoritarian view of learning. Moreover, the influence of progressive ideas on the arts in education was the promotion of self-expression and creativity as a means of enhancing 'personal growth'. The term 'personal growth' is ambiguous as it carries various connotations and associations depending on context. There is a sense in which 'personal growth' is an uncontroversial notion in that, in its broadest definition, it can be argued that it is a fundamental aim of all education. But bland assent may come at the price of any useful discrimination. If personal growth involves the development of such all-embracing qualities as self awareness, confidence, perception, ability to discriminate, moral discernment, understanding and criticality, it is not unreasonable to ask whether these attributes are of equal importance, whether they are ever in contradiction or whether they are always interpreted in the same way. What is judged to be a display of confidence by one person may appear as arrogance to another. The concept of 'personal growth' in its broadest sense says everything and nothing. As with 'creativity' it is sometimes easier to define negatively in relation to what it opposes.

In the context of education, 'personal growth' philosophies in the early twentieth century stood in opposition to narrow, authoritarian methods bent on the transfer of passive information largely through rote learning and fear. The opening sentence of Holmes (1911: 3) book *What Is and What Might Be* signalled the progressive intent, 'the function of education is to encourage growth'. He went on to stress that, 'the process of growing must be done by the growing organism, by the child, let us say, and by no one else' (ibid.: 4). The term 'personal growth' came to have negative connotations because of its association with extremes of child-centred, progressive education that took non-intervention too far. It is also became associated in the context of English teaching with naïve liberal/humanist assumptions that have been challenged by critical theory. This was the view that the individual self would grow through exposure to universal truths contained in literature (or by extension art more generally) without any recognition of the way in which meanings are constructed in social contexts (Patterson, 1992). 'Personal growth' is one of those concepts that could be added to Gadamer's (2004: 9) list of words (which includes 'art', 'history', 'the creative', 'experience') that 'we take to be self evident' but in fact 'contain a wealth of history'.

The German word *Bildung* also has a long history and is difficult to translate and define, partly because it was used in various ways by different writers, but also because it too has extended connotations. Gadamer (2004: 8) quotes Herder's basic definition, 'rising up to humanity through culture' and suggests that the term *Bildung* designates the 'properly human way of developing one's natural talents and capacities'. It is sometimes translated as 'education' even though some writers see it as 'something that is qualitatively different from education' (Varkoy, 2010: 87). Sometimes the term is dismissed as old-fashioned because 'it arose within a tradition that does not relate to today's social and cultural conditions' (ibid.: 87). For the purposes of the discussion in this chapter, the important aspect captured by the concept of *Bildung* is the idea that it integrates notions of development from within with the idea of formation through external influences.

Bildung therefore is not equivalent to 'personal growth' if the latter term simply means uninhibited freedom to develop and grow. But equally it does not mean formation in a crude, technical sense. According to Gadamer (2004: 10), 'the result of Bildung is not achieved in the manner of a technical construction, but grows out of an inner process of formation and cultivation'. To describe *Bildung* simply as personal growth would therefore be misleading if by that designation the integrated concept is oversimplified. It is only a case of 'learning through' if that concept is understood in a suitably subtle way.

Learning through the arts takes different forms and can be defined either in relation to contingent benefits or with aims that have a more direct influence on the way the arts are taught. The *learning through* approach can also be associated with the individual arts subject disciplines when the justification for teaching is provided not in terms of the art subject itself but in relation to the external cognitive and social benefits. It can be identified with either child-centred, progressive approaches where the focus is more on the personal growth of the individual or, in its more contemporary manifestation, it refers to the use of the arts to promote creative learning in other subjects.

Learning in

The *learning in* the arts concept focuses on the intrinsic rather than extrinsic benefits of engaging with the arts. It is less interested, for example, in whether the learning of music can improve cognitive development but is more focused on the value of music for its own sake. Similarly, there is less emphasis on whether the visual arts develop citizenship or make students better people but more focus on the appreciation of art itself. It is associated with traditionalist aesthetics, with a conception of the arts that emerged in the eighteenth century that sought to disassociate art from utilitarian purposes. It is thus associated with a separatist view of the arts.

There is a long and established tradition that objects to the use of art to serve extrinsic and instrumental ends. This tradition discussed in Chapter 2 has different manifestations such as 'formalism', 'aestheticism' or 'art for art's sake' and encapsulates the view that art should be valued for itself alone. It is associated with the Kantian notion of disinterestedness, a response which emphasises the appreciation of form and beauty exclusively in relation to art. Eaton (2001: 57) has described this view as 'separatist' (as opposed to 'inclusive') because it separates the aesthetic not just from the moral but from all other ends and activities, such as the 'scientific, political, religious, economic'. She criticises this view, however, and suggests that our experiences and encounters with the world and the decisions we make as a result 'do not typically come in separate packages' so that we look at the world first from one and then from another standpoint (ibid.: 62). She does not claim that aesthetic experiences or considerations are never separable from other sorts, but that 'it is *not a requirement* of the aesthetic that all other interests or concerns are blocked off or out' (ibid.: 62). However, it is precisely this separation that is central to *learning in*.

The argument for associating the separatist view with *learning in* is strong. The focus in the classroom is very much on the art-based outcomes that are 'directly related to the subject matter that an arts education was designed to teach' that 'reside in perceptions and discourse unique to the arts' (Eisner, 1998: 12). As indicated above, the distinction can lead to misconceptions. In the case of drama there was an implicit assumption that *learning in* only took place when the focus of the learning was on the more formal elements of acting, play scripts, and theatre as opposed to more process-oriented approaches (Hornbrook, 1989). However, as indicated by the Sutton Hoo example above, it is a very superficial view of dramatic form; many exponents of drama in education took the view that the art form of drama was a necessary not contingent element of the learning (Bolton, 1984). However, this complication can be set aside for the moment to focus on the general concept.

Learning in can also be clearly associated with intrinsic justification for the arts, the view that the arts should be taught for their own sake. It is a valuable antidote to more utilitarian arguments that pull the arts into the service of all sorts of extraneous outcomes that have no clear connection with the arts or aesthetic experience in education as well as in wider social contexts. For example, in a discussion of public funding for the arts, Schwartz (1995: 331) refers to the many instrumental justifications that have appeared in the literature, 'including for instance that a robust arts community increases tourist revenues; that exposure to art maximizes the citizenry's welfare (either general welfare or a special "aesthetic" welfare); and, that art has a positive, moralizing effect on a citizenry'. The intrinsic view is useful as an argument against the subjection of art to crude cost–benefit analysis. As with *learning through*, the value of the intrinsic position is easier to demarcate negatively in this way, in relation to what it opposes. It is rather more difficult to distinguish in its own right, except in very general terms, for the argument can easily become circular. In its more extreme formulation the intrinsic view admits of no questions at all about purpose which, it could be argued, is atheoretical and anti-educational.

Richmond (2009: 134) describes what appreciating art for its own sake means, 'as when, for example, we view a painting, allowing our minds freely to play over its formal design, subject matter, style and qualities of expression, finding the experience worthwhile in itself'. He goes on to say, 'for many people, art and beauty are sources of well-being and value in life that need no further justification'. The suggestion that art is 'a source of well being' is not at all unreasonable but starts to point in the direction of health education, which could be seen as an extrinsic justification. As soon as the concept 'intrinsic' is used in conjunction with words like 'benefit', 'value' or 'purpose' it seems to escape its restricting shackles, so to speak, and look towards external purposes and reasons. In some ways the notion of an 'intrinsic benefit' can be seen as a contradiction in terms.

It is easy to demarcate *learning in* from *learning through* when more obvious examples are given. The teaching of music to improve performance in maths is a clear case of *learning through*. The teaching of art that focuses solely on its formal elements and excludes any talk about purpose is clearly *learning in*. However, as the examples given show, actual cases are rarely as clear cut. As soon as we begin to talk about why art is important in, for example, helping us to understand the human condition, helping us perceive the world or giving expression to human emotion, we start to stray outside the very narrow confines of the intrinsic view. This seems to be a general case of art for personal growth which is usually seen as a case of *learning through*. The *learning in* or separatist view is hard to sustain in its strict form.

Although concepts of art changed through history with the twentieth century in particular bringing many challenges to conventional notions of how art should be conceived, the separatist view of art still holds strong sway in popular consciousness. At its most negative it is associated with elitism and snobbery. It embodies the belief that the arts belong in a special sphere separate from everyday life whose rewards are confined to a privileged few. Lyas (1997: 5) describes this conception well:

> For many, art galleries are places where stains, largely rectangular, hang on walls. Standing before these stains, other people, often with a certain kind of accent, proclaim, often in voices meant to be overheard, that looking at these stains, has given them experiences so profound that failure to have them would have left their lives impoverished. And others look and just can't see any of this, just as others can make no sense of the noises in the sonic museum of the concert hall, or resolve the words of *The Waste Land* into sense.

Dewey's (2005: 4) view, introduced in Chapter 1, of a 'museum conception of art' or 'compartmental conception of fine art' (ibid.: 6) sets art on a remote pedestal. In this conception, 'art is remitted to a separate realm, where it is cut off from that association with the materials and aims of every other form of human effort, undergoing and achievement' (ibid.: 2). The emphasis is on product rather than the experience of art. Various challenges to the traditional 'bourgeois' view of art represented by different movements such as pop, conceptual and 'found' art seem unable to escape being institutionalised and elevated to 'museum' status with a consequent weakening of their radical intent. When found objects and whimsical pieces are treated with intense reverence or accompanied by inflated explanations about their meaning, the original purpose is lost (Fleming, 2011b).

The theoretical origins of *learning in*, then, are found in the separatist view of the arts that emerged in the eighteenth century. It is often associated with high art and can easily lead to elitism in that the arts are deemed appropriate for the privileged few. In contrast the *learning through* approach can be said to be more contemporary and more democratic because it is more inclined to consider the implications for education of the wider sociocultural context. However, instead of dismissing the separatist concept of art out of hand as a historical aberration within the long history of a more inclusive view of art, it is worth asking whether there are positive insights from this view that have something to say to the contemporary world, particularly the world of education.

Space for art

Germaine Greer (2011) writing in *The Guardian* has described her attempt to explain 'what is art?' to a group of sixth-formers and suggests that both students and teacher found what she had to say confusing and surprising. She subscribes to a definition that art is 'anything an artist calls art' not dissimilar to that advocated by Carey (2005). This inclusive definition makes sense in terms of the history of attempts to define art described in Chapter 2. It does not mean that all art is necessarily good art (in fact Greer suggests that 'most art is bad') but it leaves the concept of 'art' open, ready to admit new manifestations and avoids unnecessary attempts to confine its meaning. On this inclusive view it is easier to declare that 'art is part of life' as Greer does, but importantly she goes on to say that, 'in order to be art it has to create for itself a separate zone, what we might call the art space or the art time'. This important insight makes more sense of aspects of the historical intrinsic/separatist view that, once stripped of any implications of elitism, have something important to say.

One element of this view is that it preserves the distinction between art and the broader notion of the aesthetic. This is significant for education. It is useful to recognise the family resemblance between art and the wider concept of the aesthetic that extends to nature and embraces so many aspects of life such as choosing wallpaper, picking a tie, positioning furniture, but it avoids the total dissolution of art into very broad notions of culture. A narrower rather than all-embracing concept of art makes it easier to establish what art education is trying to achieve. One aspect of the separatist view also recognises the significance of human intention in the making of art. This is not to make the mistake of thinking that intention determines meaning but recognising that art is made intentionally by human agents. Dewey (2005: 25) refers to the importance of 'directive intent' when applying the word 'art'. Wittgenstein (1998: 6) writes that 'only the artist can represent the individual thing so that it appears to us as a work of art'.

The notion of art creating its own space can also be associated with a view that sees engagement with art as paradoxically a stepping out of life's mainstream for purposes of renewal in order to engage with life more productively. Shusterman (2003) has pointed out that underlying the dichotomy between high art and low art are concepts of art and entertainment. This idea was introduced in Chapter 1 but its sphere of reference can now be extended. Although he is not writing specifically about education this insight certainly rings true in this context; there is understandably an almost paranoiac reluctance amongst advocates of arts in education to describe the arts as entertainment for fear that the notion will transmute into 'mere entertainment' thereby confirming once again that arts do not warrant more than a very minor role. The concept of entertainment has been criticised for triviality and narrowness. However, Shusterman points out that the etymology of the term 'entertainment' and attendant concepts points to a deeper meaning.

> The straightforward philosophical lesson implied by this etymology is that a good, if not necessary way, to maintain oneself is to occupy oneself pleasurably and with interest. The same idea is expressed in the term 'recreation', where one sustains oneself by reviving or recreating our energy through pleasurable activity.
>
> (Ibid.: 293)

Shusterman (ibid.: 296) explores the history of the way entertainment has been treated by a range of significant writers including Plato (who distinguished entertainment from philosophy and saw the mimetic arts as producing corruption of the soul), Montaigne (who recognised that entertainment can take demanding, meditative forms), Kant (where the notion of entertainment is used with both 'low' and 'high' connotations and for the disinterested free entertainment of the mental faculties that mark our experience of beauty) and Schiller (who insists on the ennobling value of play). This balanced view of entertainment (disturbed as Shusterman points out by Hegel's turn towards the ideal) does much to challenge a too easy dismissal of the concept of entertainment. It lends support to the view that 'we succeed and secure our physical sustenance by looking outward not inward', which is an important insight for education (ibid.: 293).

The Kantian notion of disinterestedness usually associated with the extreme separatist view in aesthetics has been described by Eagleton (2003: 134) as a 'radical political concept' and for postmodern theory 'the last word in delusion':

> Disinterestedness does not mean being magically absolved from interests, but recognising that some of your interests are doing you no good, or that it is in the interest of doing an effective job to set certain of them apart for the moment. It demands imagination, sympathy and self-discipline. You do not need to rise majestically above the fray to decide that in a specific situation, somebody else's interests should be promoted over yours.

Winston (2010: 50) draws attention to the process of 'unselfing' when we experience beauty in that we 'forget about our anxieties and out day-to-day preoccupations'. The concept of 'beauty' like that of the 'aesthetic' which fell out of favour in art and cultural theory is in the process being 'resurrected' (Kieran, 2005: 47). This is in part because it does not have to be associated with narrow forms of elitism. As Kieran (ibid.: 100) acknowledges, aesthetic tradition conceived of art as a practice distinct from other human concerns but he goes on to say that in part 'this was no bad thing since it provided a buffer against the subsumption of art by crude utilitarian, commercial and moralising purposes'.

As with so many conceptual distinctions addressed in this book, the key question is not so much how can we define 'learning in' and 'learning through' so that we can easily identify examples of each but rather how is this distinction potentially helpful for teaching the arts? The benefits and dangers of both approaches is summarised in Table 6.1 adapted from Fleming (2011b). The 'learning through' approach is in danger of moving the teaching away from the importance of form and technique. This is apparent in the use of drama across the curriculum when students are simply asked to act out a scene, say, The Prodigal Son, with little support or use of the dramatic form to focus the learning. Similarly, if the teaching of music is justified purely on the basis of 'learning through' (for example that it improves cognitive development) there is less motivation to ensure that

TABLE 6.1 Perspectives on 'learning in' and 'learning through'

	LEARNING THROUGH	LEARNING IN
DANGERS	Importance of form diminished Loss of quality Loss of identity as art Mechanical Instrumental	Separatist Traditional Essentialist Social and cultural context neglected Elitist
BENEFITS	Inclusive Embedded Purposeful Transformational	Importance of form recognised Preservation of quality Artistic integrity Skills

Adapted from Fleming (2011b).

the curriculum is suitably balanced. If the arts are subsumed into the learning objectives of other subjects the approach is in danger of becoming mechanical and restricted. On the other hand, a 'learning in' approach runs the risk of embracing a traditional, separatist conception of art that pays little heed to the social and cultural context.

However, these perceptions can be balanced by seeing the positive contribution from each side. The 'learning through' approach has potential to challenge teachers to think about purpose and aims without these becoming narrow and instrumental. In this approach, art is removed from its pedestal and embedded in real-life contexts. The 'learning in' view when considered in a more balanced way contains an implicit argument for maintaining the concept of arts in education and resisting the implicit tendency to dissolve the concept of art into creativity and culture. It is to the concept of creativity that we now turn.

Further reading

For a discussion of Kantian aesthetics, the concept of disinterestedness and a detailed guide to further reading see Chapter 1 of *Aesthetics* (Lyas, 1997). See also Wicks (2007) *Routledge Philosophy Guidebook to Kant on Judgment*. Chapter 5, 'From Aesthetics to Art Criticism', of Danto's (1997) *After the End of Art* addresses notions of the aesthetic and beauty in relation to modern art. For a discussion of the value of a rich conception of 'learning through' see Chapter 12 'Art and Life' in Best (1985) *Feeling and Reason in the Arts*. A special edition of the *Journal of Philosophy of Education* with an introduction by Lovlie and Standish (2002) was devoted to the concept of *Bildung*. See entries on 'Aestheticism' by Dowling and on 'Art for Art's Sake' by Crispin in the *Encyclopedia of Aesthetics* (Kelly, 1998). A relevant article 'Intrinsic Value and the Notion of Life' is reprinted in Levinson (2006) *Contemplating Art – Essays in Aesthetics*.

7

Creativity

Introduction

The idea for the lesson was a good one. The familiar story of *The Pied Piper* would be used as the basis for an improvised drama set in a modern context, a housing estate. Fifteen minutes into the lesson the scene is rather chaotic. Instead of the animated exchange between the mayor and residents that took place on the in-service course from which the idea came, the children have started to shriek and stamp on imaginary rats. One of them has decided he would make a good cat and is running around on all fours chasing the rats who are squeaking and making rat-like faces. Some of the rats and residents have started to fight, with one of the rats executing fancy karate moves. At a later point in the lesson when the pupils are asked to act out a scene showing a town bereft of children there is much miming of pulling champagne corks, drinking and dancing (Fleming, 2011a: 19). Much later when reflecting on the lesson, the teacher finds consolation in the fact that the class have been exercising their 'imagination' and 'creativity'. Once again these terms with their expedient lack of precision have come to the rescue as a form of self-deceptive sticking plaster.

'Creativity' illustrates extremely well the contrast between ease of use and the difficulty of arriving at a clear definition of a concept. After all, when 'creativity' is used in context it is readily understood as embracing notions of originality, inventiveness and flexibility, while standing in opposition to anything that smacks of predictability, uniformity and rigidity. In the context of education creativity involves seeing things in new ways rather than just regurgitating information that has been learned by heart. There have been fairly recent definitions of creativity that recur in the literature. In *All Our Futures* (NACCCE, 1999: 30) it is defined as 'imaginative activity fashioned so as to produce outcomes that are both original and of value'. This is not dissimilar to Sternberg and Lubart's (1999: 3) definition of creativity as 'the ability to produce work that is both novel (i.e. original, unexpected) and appropriate (i.e. useful, adaptive concerning task constraints)'. On the other hand, a number of writers have made reference to the difficulty of pinning the concept down: 'it is impossible to give a simple definition of "creativity"' (White, 1995: 88); the concept of creativity is 'ever-elusive' (Gallagher, 2007: 1229); in trying to understand the nature of creativity, 'there is little chance of finding a master formula' (Margolis, 1985: 13); it is a 'portmanteau term taking under its ambit a number of closely and some less closely related concepts, some of them incompatible or even contradictory, all vague and fuzzy at the edges' Osborne (1984: 213). This is unlikely to come as a surprise given the repeated theme in this book that meaningful language use is not dependent on precise classification.

Providing some sort of definition is not the problem. The difficulty comes rather from trying not to oversimplify the concept in doing so, with potential negative impact on practice. As with the concept of 'art', creativity has been conceived in various ways at different times and with different elements coming to the fore in importance, for example, the exclusive emphasis on genius and giftedness broadened to embrace more expansive ideas about the capability of the majority. The use of psychometric tests to establish levels of divergent thinking of the individual was later complemented by approaches that were more conscious of emotional, contextual and cultural dimensions. It is sometimes hard to find one's bearing in this area (White, 1995: 88). There have been different approaches to understanding creativity, described as mystical, psychoanalytical, pragmatic, psychometric, cognitive and social-personality (Sternberg and Lubart, 1999). This diversity adds a further challenge to the process of clarification.

The main focus in this chapter is on creativity as it pertains to the arts and specifically to arts in education. However, this discussion needs to take place in the wider context of the explosion of interest in creativity in all curriculum subjects as well as in fields beyond education. We will look first, then, at this wider context before focusing more specifically on arts education. The intention is not to conduct a comprehensive review of the literature but rather to highlight the more relevant debates. If a discussion of creativity is to be useful and more than just an intellectual spring clean it needs to uncover ways in which uses of the term may inadvertently affect practice by either limiting possibilities or extending them too far.

Questions of definition

The question 'what is creativity?' is not always the best starting point for establishing a general understanding of the term. It is not so misleading if it just implies a need for some conceptual clarification of use but it can suggest that there is a correct use of term waiting to be discovered. As Allen and Turvey (2001: 5) have pointed out in relation to Wittgenstein's view, it a mistake to try to answer questions of sense and meaning by empirical enquiry. Nor is it appropriate to look for the necessary and sufficient conditions for the use of a term which was the basic procedure for early analytic philosophy. Wittgenstein came to reject the conception of meaning he held in the *Tractatus*, that meaning is hidden from human beings and needs to be laid bare by philosophy. As he later came to see, because meaning is determined by its use in social contexts it is not hidden but it is not always clear-cut.

There are times when a narrow definition needs to be established for a particular purpose, for example when a test of creativity is being used for research purposes. However, in this case the test is assessing a construct of creativity that may only approximate to the myriad uses of the concept in real contexts. The technical research term here is 'construct validity', which seeks to establish that the construct being measured is 'correct'. However, this often necessitates an artificial narrowing with dangers of circularity in that the item being measured is by definition the 'construct' that has been created. A test of creativity always measures the construct of creativity embodied in the test – nothing more. It is important to be aware of the dangers of working with a limited concept because it may miss out elements that are important for pedagogy.

An alternative to starting with a narrow prescribed definition is to elucidate the associations that attach to the concept and those to which it is opposed. For that we need to have the sort of tolerance of ambiguity and ragged edges that is more at home with art than logic. Some of the most common associations are summarised in Table 7.1 and draw attention to resonance and texture rather than the precise referential object of the word. The concept of 'originality' in the sense of making something new appears in many definitions but it is not always clear whether the item must be original in some absolute sense or just to the creator. This has important ramifications for children's creativity if it is only important that what is new is new to the child. Originality has been a central idea in the appreciation of art, which is often thought of as original creation as opposed to craft, which, in contrast, is seen as carrying out an instruction or employing a technique. It is also easy to see how 'skill' may become detached from 'creativity' when the latter is associated with freedom and notions of breaking through conventional boundaries.

The ancient association of creativity with the idea of being inspired by a muse led to the notion of creative thought beginning with an involuntary impulse (Wilkinson, 1992: 223). In more recent thinking, the role played by the muse was taken over by the unconscious mind. Both versions reinforce the notion of creativity as being associated with sudden insight rather than emanating from a process of slow evolution of perception. Thus concepts of tradition associated with rule following, and the concept of 'wisdom' (with its overtones of discernment built up steadily through experience) sit less easily with some notions of creativity. Craft (2006: 337) has drawn attention to the fact that the interest in creativity in the wider education sphere has developed with insufficient reference to a values framework. She makes a case for nurturing creativity with wisdom in schools and emphasises responsibility as well as rights in her discussion of market-driven models of creativity in education. Creativity often has positive overtones but not always. To some it evokes notions of chaos rather than order; waste rather than efficiency;

TABLE 7.1 Creativity associations

CREATIVITY	
TENDS TOWARDS . . .	RATHER THAN . . .
Originality	Tradition
Innovation	Discovery
Freedom	Being rule-bound
Play	Skill
Individuality	Conformity
Production	Consumption
Insight	Imitation
Imagination	Wisdom

discontinuity rather than continuity thus opening up possibilities of negative associations, depending on one's perspective.

Elliott (1991) distinguished between what he termed 'traditional' and 'new' concepts of creativity. The traditional notion of creativity was associated with divine creation and placed emphasis on bringing something new into existence. It was therefore distinguished from concepts of 'discovery' and 'invention'. Scientists, for example, were thought to be engaged in discovery rather than creation. Moreover, although 'invention' was thought to belong in the same family of terms as 'creation' it is not quite the same. One of the differences is that creation is associated more with free activity, whereas both the scientist and perhaps to a lesser degree the inventor are subject to some limitations associated with functional outcomes. The newer concept of 'creativity' according to Elliott came into prominence after World War II, when the space and nuclear research projects presented problems which required imagination for their solution. The concept of creativity, evolving in relation to the social context, then become extended to embrace ideas of problem solving and getting novel ideas.

Townley and Beech (2010: 9) in their discussion of the creative industries draw attention to the antipathy which has arisen between 'creativity' and 'management' because the latter is associated with planning and organising. They question whether it is necessary or productive to see them in opposition in this way. A similar tension can be said to exist between 'creativity' and 'teaching' in that the latter is also associated with discipline, control and defined outcomes. The renewed interest in creativity in education in the UK since the publication of the NACCCE report in 1999 can be seen in part as a reaction to the decade of highly centralised, restricted curriculum driven by external assessment.

Table 7.1 summarises different concepts that may or not be evoked by the concept of creativity, whereas Table 7.2 identifies dichotomies associated with the concept. In other words, Table 7.1 summarises attempts that have been made to say both what it is and what it is not, whereas table 7.2 shows contrasting conceptions of what it is. Contemporary approaches which investigate the concept of creativity often do so by identifying key dichotomies (NACCCE, 1999; Banaji et al., 2010). The notion of 'creative genius' is associated with Kant's (1928: 168) views according to which, the artistic genius is a 'talent for producing that for which no definite rule can be given: and not an aptitude in the way of cleverness for what can be learned according to some rule'. His doctrine of artistic creativity became 'the cornerstone of Romanticism' (Crawford, 2001: 61). Creativity is characterised as natural talent or natural gift and, once again, it is easy to see how there

TABLE 7.2 Creativity dichotomies

Genius	Ubiquitous
Elite	Democratic
Cannot be taught	Can be taught
Personal	Social
Separatist	Inclusive
Brings something new	Does not necessarily bring something new
Intrinsic to humanity	Extrinsic to humanity
Convergent	Divergent

may be a tension between 'creativity' and 'teaching'. Furthermore, on this view only a minority are said to be creative leading to notions of elitism. As the NACCCE report (1999: 28) points out, 'the literature of creativity often focuses on the great men and women who have produced or made path-breaking compositions, paintings, inventions or theories'.

Banaji *et al.* (2010: 29) provide an account of the more 'ubiquitous' conception of creativity which takes the view that small 'c' creativity is manifest in everyday experience in meeting the demands of living. On this view, everyone has the potential for creativity. It is associated with the democratic concept, which tends to be opposed to the elitism of high art (Willis, 1990). There are echoes here of the ideas of inclusiveness and separatism discussed in Chapter 6. As suggested there, it is not a simple matter of making a simple choice between these extremes, nor is it appropriate to say that such dichotomies are unhelpful (NACCCE, 1999: 9). What they do is alert us to possibilities and dangers that need to be interpreted in context with a view to practice.

There has been a surge of interest in creativity in education and creative approaches to learning in the UK which, as suggested above, has arisen as a backlash against years of a very restricted approach to the curriculum. It thus has picked up on the view 'that current priorities and pressures in education inhibit the creative abilities of young people and of those who teach them' (NACCCE, 1999: 8). As Sefton-Green *et al.* (2011: 2) point out, the term 'creative learning' has two meanings: 'teaching for creativity' or 'teaching creatively', but these notions are related because the intention in both is similar.

> At its most basic, the idea of creative learning stands in opposition to a steady diet of teacher directed, atomised and reductive worksheets, quizzes, exercises and tests, many of which render the teacher a mere delivery agent for a syllabus developed elsewhere. In this context, creative learning is an experimental, destabilising force; it questions the starting-points and opens up the outcomes of curriculum. It makes the school permeable to other ways of thinking, knowing, being and doing.
>
> (Ibid.: 2)

At its best, creativity in education stands against all that is dull, dreary, mechanistic, insipid, uninspiring and retrograde. At its worst it is a concept that can be used to legitimise any kind of practice just because it is different without any sense of overall purpose, direction, positive discipline and sustained application. These different uses of creativity are helpful when considering arts education more specifically.

Creativity in arts in education

Much general writing on the arts does not pay much attention to creativity and when it does the word 'creation' rather than 'creativity' is more common. In contrast creativity has figured prominently in writing on arts in education. In Chapter 3 reference was made to Abbs' (1987) analysis of changing paradigms. Put simply, this was a development from a restricted notion of self expression and creativity to a broader view of arts education that encompassed responding and evaluation as well, and recognised the value of tradition. The tendency to associate 'creativity' with 'making' means that arts education was (and to some extent still is) predominantly seen in terms of creating works. Creativity and self-expression were also associated with the expression of emotions, whereas the broader, more inclusive concept of the arts (Abbs' second paradigm) placed more emphasis on cognition. This idea of expressing something externally that has its origins internally was central to the early expressionist theories and is associated with the idea that creativity is to be conceived as an internal mental process.

The problem with the conception of creativity as an internal mental process is not that it is wrong but that is potentially misleading because it tends to direct attention away from social processes and external criteria inwards to what is hidden. It evokes an image that creativity is 'secreted' unconsciously from the brain of the genius (Janik, 2001: 95). If this image dominates educational thinking it also tends to promote an elitist view. It also conceptualises the teacher's role as one which focuses largely on stimulating the inner source of creativity. Furthermore, the 'inward' view leads to the assumption that there are no criteria for judging outcomes and anything that is considered 'creative' can be valued as being worthwhile. This was the case with the example given at the start of this chapter.

The focus on process and experience at the expense of the product helped to reinforce the view that any kind of evaluation of quality was inappropriate. Moreover, the prioritising of the internal and private over the external and public led in some cases to a suspicion of the teaching of techniques as well as the neglect of form and the aesthetic dimensions of art.

As we saw in Chapter 2, the focus in art theory moved from the author (associated with romanticism) to the work of art itself and then to the audience or reader, with more attention to how the work was being received. Insights from reception and reader-response theorists strengthen the view that creativity in art does not only reside in making works but also lies in responding to the work of others. Once again this view is only tenable if we think 'outwardly' rather than 'inwardly'. Much of the thinking on reception and reader-response derives from literary theory but the implications are applicable to all the arts. Rosenblatt (1986) drew on Dewey's thinking, which challenged the tendency to see human beings as separate from nature, instead recognising this relationship as reciprocal and mutually defining. She applied this idea of 'transaction' to the relationship between reader and text in that the meaning does not reside solely in the text itself, but is found in the transactional process.

> Each reader brings a unique reservoir of public and private significances, the residue of past experiences with language and texts in life situations. The transaction with the signs of the text activates a two-way, or, better, circular, stream of dynamically intermingled symbolizations which mutually reverberate and merge.
>
> (Ibid.: 123)

Similar ideas are found in Gadamer (2004) who took the view that meaning is not determined solely by the intention of the author; as the work passes from one historical context to another, different meanings accrue.

Iser's (1988) phenomenological approach to reading also placed emphasis on the centrality of consciousness and the convergence of text and reader to create meaning. He thought it more appropriate to see meaning as something that *happens* not something fixed and static. In a celebrated paper, Elliott (1972) describes the importance of the imagination of the percipient (or audience) in the experience of art. A work, he suggests, may be experienced 'from within' or 'from without'. When we experience a poem from within we do not fix our attention upon it but live it according to a certain imaginative mode. He also uses an example of a painting to explain what he means:

> A picture like Rouault's 'Flight Into Egypt' would be quite insignificant if it did not have the power suddenly to make it seem that we are actually there, in an unbounded landscape, with the sky extending over us in a chill dawn. Our point of view shifts spontaneously from a point outside the world of the work to a point within it.
>
> (Ibid.: 155)

All of these authors base their view on the fact that we are not passive receivers of the world but active in 'shaping, glorifying and consummating it' (Lyas, 1997: 31). There are also implications for pedagogy. A creative response to a work of art is not generally evoked simply by a dry form of analysis or through inductive, closed question and answer. Nor is it achieved in most cases by simply asking for an expression of opinion. In recent years there has been an admirable emphasis in pedagogical thinking on pupil voice and opinion. However an emphasis on student independence should not lead to a diminution of the teacher's role in providing induction, guidance, leadership, direction and support. Interpretation according to Iser (2001) does not necessarily come naturally.

Rosenblatt (1986) refers to James's notion of 'selective attention' when certain aspects of a text are brought into awareness or pushed into the background. One important aspect of pedagogy is to judge how and when to draw attention to certain aspects of a work. Rosenblatt's distinction between an 'aesthetic' and 'efferent' reading of a text is also useful in understanding the teacher's role in helping students take up a stance in relation to the text. This involves an element of meta-awareness. An efferent stance focuses attention predominantly on what is carried away after the reading; Rosenblatt gives the example of a mother whose child has swallowed a poisonous liquid who reads the label with a specific narrow purpose. In contrast, a predominantly aesthetic stance designates an attitude of readiness to focus on what is being lived through in relation to the text during the reading event.

Interpretation, then, is not equivalent to translation or explanation but takes a more subtle form. So too is the process of teaching response to art. This may involve helping learners engage with the work by relating the art object to their own experience, making comparisons, highlighting some aspects more than others. It is a subtle process in which the teacher must decide when explanation is appropriate and when it is not, to ensure a balance between authentic and informed response.

Although, as described earlier, there are dangers in the use of creativity in the context of art education, this does not mean that it should have no place. Seeing response to art as a creative process is one example of how the term can be useful. Its value goes further. As Elliot (1991: 70) has said, the concept can function as a 'regulative idea' in education, as 'a focus of human hopes and aspirations'. It has for him an 'inspirational force' and is a reminder that education is concerned with ideas of innovation and progress: 'it proclaims the strength of the spirit against necessity'.

Further reading

The series of literature reviews commissioned by Creative Partnerships are concise and readable: Banaji *et al.* (2010) *Rhetorics of Creativity*; Bragg (2007) *Consulting Young People*; Thomson (2007) *Whole School Change*; O'Connor (2010) *Creative and Cultural Industries*; Jewitt (2008) *The Visual in Learning and Creativity*; Marsh (2010) *Childhood, Culture and Creativity*; Jones (2009) *Culture and Creative Learning*; Oakley (2009) *Art Works: Cultural Labour Markets*. They are available online (www.creative-partnerships.com/research-resources/research/literature-reviews,73,ART.html).

Kaufman and Sternberg's (eds) (2006) *The International Handbook of Creativity* provides a range of international perspectives on the psychology of human creativity, highlighting similarities and differences. See also Kaufman and Baer (eds) (2006) *Creativity and Reason in Cognitive Development*. There is a section of collected papers on creativity in Bresler (ed.) (2007) *International Handbook of Research in Arts Education* with a useful overview by Burnard. For other relevant texts see Kaufman and Sternberg (eds) (2010) *The Cambridge Handbook of Creativity*; Robinson (2001) *Out of Our Minds: Learning to Be Creative*; Sefton-Green and Sinker (eds) (2000) *Evaluating Creativity: Making and Learning by Young People*; Sefton-Green (ed.) (1999) *Creativity, Young People, and New Technologies: The Challenge of Digital Arts*.

8

Assessment

Introduction

In 2009 the Arts Council in the UK announced a new nationwide scheme for artistic assessment of regularly funded organisations, starting in 2010. They proposed to ask a range of informed people to view individual pieces of artistic activity (a show or an exhibition or a publication, for example) and write a report assessing the work's artistic achievement. To some commentators steeped in the technical issues of educational assessment this approach might seem to be rather subjective, lacking any robust basis for reliability and impartiality. It will be the argument of this chapter that such criticisms are misguided and that the underlying philosophical and theoretical principles of this sort of approach are entirely sound. Moreover, the same principles that apply to evaluation of artistic programmes can be applied to assessment in schools.

Perhaps more than any other issue in education, assessment causes tension and differences of opinion because the form it takes exercises considerable influence on teaching and the curriculum. At its worst, standardised testing, because it often has such huge implications for schools, may result in the narrowest forms of 'teaching to the test'. In arts in education the complexities and challenges are often thought to be greater because, whereas assessment strives towards precision, certainty and predictability, the arts are more ready to embrace ambiguity and uncertainty. In most countries the arts in education have to function in a contemporary culture of assessment with an increasing emphasis on clear learning outcomes, targets and testing; it is therefore important to recognise the potential limiting effects of those pressures but also consider how the arts can best operate in this kind of context.

Terms such as assessment, evaluation, testing and monitoring are often used interchangeably or with different nuances in different countries. 'Evaluation', for example, is sometimes used in relation to judging the overall effectiveness of institutions or courses, including arts programmes. The term is also used when seeking to provide information on average levels of proficiency in regions or countries. It is possible to do this by a process of sampling rather than by using summative data derived from an entire population as long as the system is not obsessed with singling out the results of individual schools. When assessment data is used to compare the progress of different cohorts of pupils, the use of a 'value-added' approach which takes account of the different base-lines from which the pupils are progressing is becoming more common. The primary focus in this chapter, however, is not so much on evaluating programmes or achievement at a national level but on making a judgement on the extent to which pupils' learning has been successful. This is a challenge for all subjects.

The Norwood report of 1943 condemned outright the examination of children in art. 'These subjects which depend so greatly upon individual genius and taste cannot in our view be brought at the school stage within the confines of external examination, however sympathetically devised' (Secondary School Examinations Council, 1943: 275). Writing in 1978, Ross felt concern about the damaging effects that exam pressure can have on the arts but took the view 'since we cannot beat them we may have to join them' (ibid.: 265). These views were not untypical. However, contemporary approaches to assessment extend beyond examinations and tests. Even so, it is often felt that the arts are a special case when it comes to matters of assessment compared with other subjects.

There is perhaps a danger of over-emphasising the differences between the concerns and preoccupations within assessment in the arts and those that belong to the wider educational sphere. After all, the difficulties involved in judging and appraising works of art have been frequently addressed in art theory (Croce, 1992: 132; Sibley, 1959) often with an emphasis on reconciling issues related to subjectivity and objectivity. Hume (2002) in *Of the Standard of Taste* asked why there is such varied taste in the world and sought to explain that variety and how we arrive at judgements that have some claim to objectivity and universality. The issue of taste in mainstream aesthetics remains 'alive and controversial' (Korsmeyer, 2001: 201). For this reason it may be appropriate not just to consider the problem posed by the challenge of assessment in arts education but to ask whether issues related to judgement and evaluation in the arts can illuminate assessment in education more generally.

This chapter, then, will begin with an overview of more general issues in assessment, focusing in particular on the wide range of functions that assessment is intended to fulfil before relating these specifically to the arts. It is often claimed that only more superficial and surface learning can be subject to assessment and what is more important is impossible to assess. This question needs to be addressed in the context of a consideration of internal and external dimensions of experience, and notions of subjectivity and objectivity; for if something is internal it is by definition hidden, and if judgements are largely subjective how can they be reliable? The chapter will conclude with a consideration of broader assessment issues as they pertain to the teaching of the arts, as well as whether the arts can inform debates in education. The tension between analytic and synthetic ways of experiencing the world is highly relevant to all of these issues.

Assessment issues

Somewhat paradoxically, assessment tends to cause most confusion when there is a failure to recognise its complexities. At its simplest, the role of assessment is to provide information on whether teaching/learning has been successful. However, there a number of potential different audiences for that information whose requirements pull in different directions. Classroom teachers need to know how students' knowledge, skills and understanding are developing. Such formative information is valuable so they can adjust their teaching and determine what kind of feedback is needed to improve performance. Headteachers and governments, on the other hand, need additional, broader information on the quality of education in a school or country (as suggested above, this is sometimes called evaluation or monitoring). The data required for this purpose needs a high level of reliability and uniformity; we need to feel confident that an 'A' grade in one region means the same elsewhere. Employers and society at large also need reliable information which can help select people either for jobs or for the next stage of their education. Parents too require information which can help them understand their children's achievements and limitations. Learners themselves need to know how they are progressing and how to improve their performance but they may need to be protected from being demotivated by too much negative assessment.

The different purposes related to the different potential audiences illustrate the challenge involved in devising assessment instruments. Of course the situation as described refers to how things are in most developed countries, not how they necessarily ought to be. Arguably the use of the term 'need' in the preceding paragraph is open to question but this is generally how the situation is, and an element of pragmatism is needed when determining what stance to take on assessment of arts subjects. The account shows two central tendencies emerging. One places emphasis on the need for reliable, objective measures. In practice the making of summative judgements is likely to involve more formal examinations and tests with mark schemes to ensure that the process is sound. An alternative approach is to change the emphasis from assessment *of* learning to assessment *for* learning, implying a more formative approach where there is much more emphasis on feedback to improve performance. The approach here might be through course work and portfolio assessment in which diverse information can be gathered which reflects the true broad nature of the subject. The broader the approach to assessment (incorporating the judgement of a range of different performances in different contexts) the more it can be said to constitute a meaningful assessment of performance in the subject. However, tension emerges because it is sometimes difficult to compare, with any degree of accuracy, the results drawn from broad approaches to assessment. It is the quest for 'objective' and reliable methods of assessment driven by narrow ideas of accountability that can lead to a narrow curriculum and poor, over-directive teaching.

These different approaches based on the functions of assessment are widely recognised and are more helpful in understanding the challenges presented by assessment in the arts than the view which places undue emphasis on the differences between the arts and other subjects. It is often claimed that maths and science are easier to assess because there is such a thing as a 'correct answer'. There is a small element of truth in this statement but it presents a rather reductive view of these subjects and fails to recognise the importance of assessing understanding. There is an element of factual knowledge required in maths and science, but that is only one element of the total picture, and the same can be said of arts subjects. For example, in music we may want assess pupils' knowledge of musical notation, but this is only one small element of their achievement in music. Some of the key themes that have emerged in this book in other chapters can help to illuminate difficulties involved in assessing all subjects, not just the arts: the nature of language and meaning, the distinction between process and product and the recognition of analytic and synthetic distinctions.

Assessment criteria to guide assessment are often written with a tacit belief that language is transparent, with an assumption that if the criteria are specific and detailed enough, there will be no room for disagreement or misinterpretation. Thus assessment schemes sometimes become more and more detailed in an attempt to dispel ambiguity. However, this view ignores the fact that the meaning of language is not static and frozen but is negotiated in context. A simple descriptor in music such as, 'Pupils recognise and explore the ways sounds can be combined and used expressively' does not tell us much on its own without interpretation through sharing examples. An attempt to make it exact by trying to pin down the exact meaning of 'recognise' or 'expressively' is not just impracticable but theoretically unsound. Trying to formulate language achievement and progression in simple statements is difficult because so much is necessarily left unsaid. For example, in assessing language competence, the claim that a learner can 'write a letter' does not say whether the intended language use is formal or informal, whether the subject matter is familiar or unfamiliar, or whether the key focus is pragmatic communication or accuracy. A partial solution is to make the statements of learning outcomes more complex and nuanced (e.g. 'can write an informal letter to a friend on a familiar topic at a level of accuracy that does not inhibit communication') but this process, when extended to a whole range of statements, can detract from their practical utility because they become too complex. There is a compromise to be found between brevity and simplicity on the one hand and expansion and complexity on the other (Fleming, 2006a).

This suggests that assessment is rarely a precise process and almost always involves some level of approximation. When criteria are developed they need to be used with caution as their effectiveness is likely to depend on interpretation through negotiation within communities of practice. It is important to guard against formulating criteria that provide merely the illusion of common understanding and agreement with no basis in actual practice. There is a similar challenge in trying to assess what a pupil has written for assessment purposes, particularly in an examination context where the individual is unknown to the examiner. Determining levels of understanding always involves a degree of inference. For that reason some insight into process can help inform judgements about the product.

Arts practitioners are familiar with the concepts of 'product' and 'process' and the distinction is useful for assessment. When faced simply with a product such as an essay written in examination conditions it is not always easy to determine how much has been written from rote recall or to what degree the candidate is manipulating language without any deep understanding. (In fact it may be tempting to argue that when evaluating products within the arts such as a sculpture or painting the task is actually less difficult because of the absence of the confounding effects of language.) The convention of having an oral examination at doctoral level to accompany the assessment of a written product, the thesis, is to provide some insight into the process and in part to guarantee both ownership and understanding. Occasionally there is public outrage that examinations or national tests in different subjects need to be re-marked because the original results proved to be unreliable. However, given the complexity of what is being assessed in the contemporary curriculum, and given that examiners are, for practical reasons, largely restricted to focusing more on a de-contextualised product, it is perhaps more surprising that any semblance of reliability is achieved at all. The research and development workers of exam boards, test developers and national organisations are constantly seeking new ways of refining procedures; good assessment is challenging in all subjects, not just the arts, and techniques are evolving.

In any assessment scheme there is a need to break down broad concepts into constituent components. However, it is the degree of precision required that is often the subject of dispute. As indicated in the examples given above, the move from a broad, synthetic approach to assessment to a more analytic description of precise learning goals brings dangers. Important aspects that are implicit in the broad concept may be lost when translated into more atomised statements; in this case, the whole is not necessarily exactly equivalent to the sum of the parts. There also may be an effect on the teaching which, as a consequence of the atomised approach, becomes episodic and mechanistic. This distinction between the analytic and synthetic is helpful in thinking about assessment. Analytic schemes may be useful but they must remain as 'emissary' (or servant), not 'master' (McGilchrist, 2009). In other words, it is important not to become overwhelmed by the mechanics and details of the process and lose sight of overall vision and purpose. In practice, holistic human judgement inevitably comes into all but the narrowest forms of assessment.

Exploring dichotomies

Contemporary teaching, learning and assessment largely deals in 'outcomes', or what is 'external'. However, what is 'internal' is of particular importance to the arts and it is from this insight that the claim is often made that the arts are either completely incompatible or hard to reconcile with assessment. Writing about drama, Taylor (2000: 74) takes issue with educators who have tried to fit the dynamic curriculum into an outcome-oriented programme that focuses on skills and attitudes that can be measured rather than 'the intrinsic changes which happen inside humans when they experience a work of art'. Clark and Goode (1999: 13) point out that the drama process is 'a mediation between our inner selves and the real world'. It is easy to sympathise with these sentiments because the arts are undoubtedly concerned with our internal lives; the contribution of progressive and romantic thinking was to ensure that depth of feeling, emotion, engagement and authenticity were given due attention in arts education. The problem, however, is that the polarisation between the external and the internal can be envisaged too starkly. We seem to be torn between subscribing to a form of behaviourism (whereby only external actions are considered important) or to some sort of romantic mysticism.

Assessment that attempts to go beyond surface notions of simple propositional knowledge and probes dimensions important to the arts such as commitment, engagement and creativity is a challenge, but is it actually impossible? Behind this question lie two competing explanations of the nature of human beings and in particular the relationship between mind and body. One view is that there are aspects of a human being that are hidden from external scrutiny, that are only subject to internal introspection to which only the subject has direct access. The other view is that there is no internal dimension, that everything lies on the surface. Overgaard (2007: 5) expresses the attraction of the two competing positions and the tension between them:

On the one hand, we are inclined to think that it is wrong to claim, as Cartesian dualists would have to do, that the minds of others are essentially inaccessible to direct experience. But on the other hand we feel that it is equally wrong to claim, as behaviorists have done, that the mental lives of subjects are completely accessible to an outside spectator.

The distinction arises in the context of assessment because if we give credence and value to what is essentially hidden and private this makes any attempt at justification or evaluation invalid. However, if we do not value what is internal we seem to occupying very arid and reductive territory, the antithesis of what the arts stand for. The key to resolving this issue is to turn attention to the way language is used. Wittgenstein's writing is helpful precisely because of its focus on language, an emphasis that is often missed in discussion about 'inner processes' in relation to art.

The grammar of the language misleadingly conveys the idea that words like 'understanding' and 'intention' refer to something that is largely internal. Many other words in our language such as 'thinking', 'feeling', 'imagining' also seem to point inwards. 'Understanding', for example, seems obviously to be a 'mental process' and is often defined as such. We speak of thoughts 'crossing one's mind' or of 'grasping the gist of what someone is saying' as if these are internal events. The inspired insight of Wittgenstein was not as much to say that this statement is wrong, for to do that would be baffling because it is counter-intuitive. What Wittgenstein (1958: 61) says is 'try not to think of understanding as a mental process at all' because that way of thinking has misleading consequences. When we ask whether someone has understood x we can only properly answer that question by observing how they act and listening to what they say. A word like 'understanding' or 'feeling' gains meaning not internally by reference to something hidden but outwardly in social contexts. An example will help elucidate this point. If we need to determine whether someone really intended to hurt us by a remark they made, it does not make sense to say that we could resolve the matter if only we had direct access to their consciousness and could look inside at their 'real' intention or motive (Fleming, 2009). Instead we confirm their intention by looking at further evidence from the patterns in their lives, from the way they live. For example, do they carry on as normal in their behaviour or is this remark one of a pattern? If we want to say a pupil read a poem with feeling we make that judgement on what we have seen and heard. That is not, however, to deny that people have 'internal lives'. Overgaard (2007: 11) employs the term 'embodiment' to capture the rich sense of what subjectivity entails; we do feel the need to thicken explanations of behaviour by reference to the 'inside' or what is 'behind' the ever present subject (ibid.: 11), 'the bodily behaviour of another subject is itself, as it were, soaked with meaning' (ibid.: 14).

It is in this sense that Finch (1995: 77) can rightly say that Wittgenstein did away with the 'house of cards' of the 'inner world' but kept a place for 'the inner life' (ibid.: 75). To repeat the key practical point, when we make an assessment we can only make judgements based on what we observe, on what we can see or what we can read or hear. In one sense this statement is so true and blindingly obvious that is seems hardly worth stating. But there is also a sense in which the statement can disturb because it seems potentially arid and restrictive, appearing to exclude elements that are key to meaningful assessment in arts such as 'personal response', 'authenticity' and 'feeling'. However, on the basis of the above discussion, in order to make such judgements we do not have to look internally but rather horizontally to the wider context. This is what makes knowledge of process as well as product helpful in these cases. On this view, it makes perfect sense to judge whether pupils are engaged in a drama performance with an appropriate level of level of feeling. Faced with a painting produced by a pupil which we are required to assess it helps to know something about the context, how the task was set, what criteria if any were set, in what ways the pupil was prepared. Attempting to judge the product in isolation can be seen as a form of unhelpful separatism.

This discussion makes it clearer why the question for assessment is not so much whether there are certain elements that are impossible to assess but whether such elements can be assessed in a reasonably straightforward way. The decision becomes more pragmatic rather than based on misleading theory. These insights have important consequences for arts education. If such words as 'feeling', 'appreciating' and 'imagining' are wrongly thought to be essentially internal and hidden then this leads us in the wrong direction and renders them irrelevant to judging outcomes. We exclude them from assessment processes but also in our teaching we escape from any responsibility for what happens on the inside, so to speak; we are freed from any accountability and responsibility for such elements. As discussed in the preceding chapter, there are obvious dangers when concepts like 'creativity' and 'imagination' become blanket terms that are used to justify any activity on the grounds that they are internal and subjective and not subject to further scrutiny.

The tension between subjectivity and objectivity has tended to inhibit the making of judgements about art and is also relevant to issues of assessment. The discussion of this issue by Lyas (1997) introduced in Chapter 3 is illuminating and well worth reading in its entirety. The terms 'objective' and 'subjective' are seductive because they seem to point to clear corresponding instances in the world: there are objects such as trees and clouds as well as subjects that have a psychological life. 'To say a strawberry has a certain mass is to say something objective. To say one likes the taste of strawberries is to say something subjective' (ibid.: 113). However, problems arise if we reduce aesthetic judgements simply to matters of liking and disliking. There is a tendency to do this in the popular expressions 'I may not know much about art but I know what I like' or 'there is no arguing with taste'. However, it is important to recognise that aesthetic judgements are judgements which relate to features in the art object rather than in the person responding; there is a difference between saying that one likes something and saying that a painting has grandeur or that a dance has elegance (ibid.: 113). The key to illuminating the subjectivity/objectivity dilemma is to recognise that statements saying that a painting has grandeur and that it contains a great deal of the colour red are more similar than appears on the surface. This needs more explanation.

Our so-called objective knowledge is always in some sense 'provisional' and 'contingent'. To some critics describing the colour as red might be wildly misleading. As Lyas (1997: 123) says, few people can see the difference between BS2100 and BS2101 on the colour chart. It is not necessary to deny the existence of truth or to subscribe to relativism. We do not actually *make* the objective world as some extreme forms of constructivism claim but we hold particular beliefs as true until such times as there is evidence to challenge them. We need a concept of truth to operate in the word, and as Wittgenstein (1969a: 13) has argued, the difference between the concept of 'knowing' and the concept of 'being certain' is not of any great importance at all. 'We are quite sure of it' does not mean just that every single person is certain of it, but that we are asserting that we belong to a community which is 'bound together'. Eagleton (2003: 103) makes a similar point when he says that the concept of 'absolute truth' adds nothing to the concept of 'truth'. Attempts to find truth do not rule out the possibility of doubt, ambiguity or being mistaken.

This means that statements about the physical world and statements about art are not so diametrically opposed because they are both based on agreement in judgement in particular contexts. Lyas (1997: 128) suggests that to make a remark about whether one likes a work of art or not is not the end of the matter but the beginning. The next stage is for someone to ask why and to enter into a dialogue:

> One says to a friend … I like the way she played the adagio. These are not subjective remarks, if to be a subjective remark is to be offered in a way that brooks no argument. These remarks are attempts to engage with another. They invite replies like, 'Yes, wasn't it good?' or 'I couldn't see much in it. What did you like about it?'; 'No, I thought Brendel did it better. Too much right hand'. In these contexts the question whether our remarks are objective or subjective simply does not arise for us.

It is in this sense that general thinking about making judgements about art can inform assessment because the process is similar. When we ascribe a grade A to a project we are not operating a fool-proof method but reaching out in an effort to establish community, to invite discussion, to get people to see things as we do. Postmodern relativism which tends to loom over discussions of art education is entirely unhelpful. We do say that some things are better than others and that is a fundamental basis for assessment. What are the practical consequences of this discussion? Assessment is both inevitable and valuable, and art education needs to embrace it for educational not just political and pragmatic reasons. We can be bolder in what we claim can be assessed. A key to achieving some semblance of reliability is in the moderation of judgements, not just the accuracy of criteria and mark schemes.

Assessing the arts

This discussion so far has placed more emphasis on the similarities between assessment in the arts and other subjects. Assessment will inevitably be based on a selection rather than the entire curriculum but the way in which a subject is assessed often draws attention to what is considered valuable. For example, 'the manner in which musical achievement is defined and assessed inevitably articulates a set of philosophical and political principles about the nature and purpose of learning, the subject being assessed and the relationship between school and society' (Spruce, 2001: 118). It is therefore helpful to distinguish programmes of study from assessment targets. This terminology was introduced as part of the National Curriculum framework in the UK to distinguish between the content of the syllabus and the focus of the assessment; in most cases not all of the syllabus can be assessed and some compromises on validity are inevitable. On the other hand, teaching may be skewed in particular unhelpful directions if the assessment process does not reflect key priorities. For example, in the arts a decision needs to be taken on the relative emphasis on making, interpretation and responding. The assessment of dance may want to see evidence not just of ability to perform but also of the type of understanding that is pertinent to appreciating dance, which may include knowledge of technical skills. Pupils may be asked to show evidence that they are able to evaluate and improve performance. Drama came under criticism in the 1990s because of what was seen as an over-emphasis on improvisation with insufficient attention to performing and responding which now appear in most assessment schemes.

Oreck (2007: 343) describes multiple forms of assessment used to evaluate student work and progress, including 'direct observation of students in class, audition or stage settings; self-reflection and self- assessment using interview, discussion and portfolios; peer response and assessment and writing testing of knowledge'. Imaginative and varied approaches to assessment that are designed to enhance the validity of judgements do not easily meet the demand for reliability, and a decision has to made about educational priorities.

It is widely recognised that art subjects do not lend themselves easily to narrow, single terminal assessment in the form of examinations. When assessing the products of students' art making we need to take into account contextual factors such as the nature of the task, the age of the students, the degree of scaffolding or support that has been provided. Portfolio assessment has a number of advantages for the arts (and in other subjects). For example, it can motivate and empower the learner, it can provide samples of performance collected over time, evidence of use and awareness of process. Portfolio assessment incorporates evidence derived from more realistic tasks in meaningful contexts, rather than relying on artificial, decontextualised tasks undertaken in timed conditions. A further advantage of this approach is that it can embody different forms of self-assessment which can also be helpful ways of motivating learners and having them reflect on their progress. The difficulty with portfolio assessment if it is conceived *only* as the accumulation of evidence produced in informal settings is, again, that it does not easily satisfy demands for reliability. Work which has been produced over an extended period of time, with formative guidance from the teacher and collaboration with classroom peers is not always seen as convincing evidence of competence.

A key concept is embodied in the notion of 'transparency', the view that those being assessed are aware of the criteria which are being used to make judgements about them and how those judgements are made. Knowledge of criteria can help performance and improve motivation but once again the issues are more complex than they first seem. A common assumption is that pupils learn best when they know what they are trying to achieve and why. While this view is largely true, there are exceptions. Learners do not always need to be fully focused on specific aspects of their performance in order to improve. In fact too much focal awareness on performance can make them too self-conscious: actors can appear too groomed and artificial; the writer who has been told to strive for effect by using more adjectives may develop a highly artificial and awkward style. These insights do not negate the importance of transparency as a principle but highlight the fact that in pedagogical practice the principle needs to be interpreted and implemented with care.

Asserting the similarity between assessment in the arts and elsewhere does not mean there are not particular challenges associated with the arts. One obvious example is that very often dance, drama and music rely on group rather than individual projects and assessment more often focuses on individual achievement. Another challenge is to how to capture non-verbal activity – mime, music, visual image (Murphy and Esspeland, 2007: 339). Improved technology is helping in this regard.

Given the dense discussion in some of this chapter it may be helpful, at the risk of oversimplification, to distil some of the key issues.

- Assessment in the arts matters not just for political reasons but to enhance educational outcomes.
- The general movement in educational thinking in the last 10 years towards assessment for learning, emphasising validity over reliability, is an encouraging development that reflects thinking in arts education assessment.
- It makes more sense to stress the similarities rather than the differences between assessing arts and other subjects.
- It is not assessment itself that is undesirable but sometimes the *use* made of assessment.
- It is important to be aware of the negative consequences for teaching of some approaches to assessment.
- We need to recognise the different functions of assessment and not assume that one scheme will fit all.
- We need to be prepared to embrace the concept of 'good enough' assessment and acknowledge there may be some rough edges when judgements are made.
- It is important to be bold in the claims made for what can be assessed and not avoid certain words as being too 'subjective'.
- The arts should not eschew descriptors and criteria – these are a valuable tool and a focus for dialogue.
- Agreement in standards evolves through dialogue, not by refining of criteria to get them 'perfect'.
- Although assessment criteria and mark schemes are important – moderation of judgements is a key process in assessment.

This discussion has inevitably been undertaken in general terms. However, in making judgements about the assessment in the arts as in other areas it is important to recognise that the different subjects have different requirements. It is to the individual arts subjects that we now turn.

Further reading

For books on general issues in assessment see Black (1998) *Testing: Friend or Foe? Theory and Practice of Testing and Assessment*; Black et al. (2003) *Assessment for Learning: Putting It Into Practice*; Broadfoot (1996) *Education, Assessment and Society*; Gipps (1994) *Beyond Testing*; Stobart (2008) *Testing Times*. Eisner (2002) has a chapter 'The Educational Uses of Assessment and Evaluation in the Arts' in his *The Arts and the Creation of Mind*. Eisner and Day's (2004) *Handbook of Research and Policy in Art Education* has a section 'Forms of Assessment in Art Education' that has five chapters by different authors on assessment in visual art. See also Boughton et al.'s (1996) *Evaluating and Assessing the Visual Arts in Education*.

9

Different arts subjects

Introduction

Some years ago I worked on a short-term project in partnership with a teacher in a primary school. We planned to do some work on poetry, specifically *The Highwayman*, a text chosen by the teacher. I had not read the poem for some years and was a bit taken aback by some of its content. At one point in the poem the landlord's daughter is gagged by the kings' men and bound to the foot of her bed with a musket propped suggestively under her breast. She manages to reach the trigger and shoot herself as a means of warning her lover, the highwayman, that a trap had been set for him. I mentioned my slight misgivings to the class teacher who reassured me that 'they' didn't bother about that sort of thing but focused instead on the alliteration, onomatopoeia, metaphors and adjectives. I was reminded of that incident when reflecting on what to include under the heading 'different art forms'. Poetry is usually found within the 'language as subject' curriculum but viewing it primarily as an art form would do much to prevent such narrow and reductive approaches to texts. This choice of poem also illustrates the folly of assuming that such categories as 'poetry' and 'fiction' are clear-cut; the poem has a strong narrative content and has been published as a song. As with 'art' itself it is not possible to place clear boundaries around the different forms and genres.

Despite the openness and indeterminacy of the word 'art', it does have coherence and value as a concept in the modern world. In education, therefore, it makes sense to group the arts subjects as a distinct category as long as we guard against the mistaken assumption that experience of being taught one or two art subjects is enough to stand for all of them. This can happen when the arts are blocked together on the curriculum to offer choice. The issue was a matter of some debate in the UK in the 1990s when Best (1995) in particular argued strongly against the view that the arts should be seen as a 'generic' group.

Best pointed out that some administrators have a vested interest in subscribing to this view because it can save on staff and timetable space. His counter arguments were partly based on asserting differences in structure (that an understanding of the structure of Bach's *A Musical Offering* is not the slightest help in understanding the structure of Picasso's *Guernica*, Tolstoy's *Anna Karenina* or Arthur Miller's *Death of a Salesman*). He also questioned the commonly held assumption that in the arts one is developing knowledge and understanding of a special and distinct kind, a view which he suggested had been advanced by notable writers including Abbs (1992). Best's assertion was that in learning to play the harp and learning to paint, something different is going on in each case. Best was also careful to make it clear that he was not arguing against cooperation and integration amongst art subjects but was questioning the logical grounds of assuming that they necessarily formed a generic community and therefore should be planned for collectively on the curriculum.

It is perfectly reasonable to be struck by the resemblances between the arts as it is to highlight their differences. What is more important than trying to determine or challenge universal categories is to explore specific consequences. One of Best's concerns was justifiably highly pragmatic, of ensuring sufficient curriculum time for all the arts. In order to advance that cause it is less important to argue over whether the arts form a generic group or offer logically distinct forms of understanding but rather more important to highlight the distinct *value* of each of the art forms. This will be one of the underlying themes of this chapter.

Another contested issue is that of determining what counts as an 'art subject' in the curriculum. This chapter will draw in part on Fleming (2010) *Arts in Education and Creativity* but it has also learned from that publication. When it came out, the editor received a complaint from one reader that in the section on the individual art forms there was no place for literature, including poetry. She had a point. That publication had followed the precedent set in the UK in official policy documents and the national curriculum in choosing art, dance, drama and music as the main art forms (OfSTED, 1998). *The Gulbenkian Report* (Robinson, 1989), however, had included literature alongside the other arts. In Australia the draft art curriculum identifies five art forms including dance, drama, media arts, music and visual arts. There is much overlap but interesting differences in these approaches. Literature and poetry are invariably part of the language curriculum and therefore often excluded from consideration as arts. Drama sometimes occupies a strange position of being both part of literature and a separate art subject with the odd consequence that studying play texts like Shakespeare tended not to be seen as part of the drama as subject curriculum. Dance is often located within physical education and 'media' seen as a separate area of study.

Deciding what counts as an arts subject is just one challenge for curriculum designers. Another issue is to decide where the boundaries are drawn in determining what counts as appropriate content within a particular art subject. Erosion of the distinction between high and low art, and subscribing to an inclusive rather than separatist conception of the arts means that there are arguments for including photography, sculpture and architecture within visual arts. There are also practical decisions to be made whether film belongs in visual art, drama, fiction or media. Increasingly the arts are taught in an integrated way. It is not the intention of this chapter to make recommendations about how the arts curriculum should be organised. This is a question for particular local contexts. Instead the emphasis will be on examining the key arts subjects and their importance as well as the key contentious issues that have surfaced in their history. One of the aims will be to show how various themes that have emerged in the book can inform thinking about specific art subjects. The categorisation adopted in this chapter is therefore fairly arbitrary.

When Lyas (1997: 2) discusses the way humans fulfil themselves aesthetically, he distinguishes between the categories of the fictional, visual and musical. Identifying a separate category of the fictional is appealing because it brings together novels, short stories, films, theatre, and television dramas, usefully eroding notions of high and low art. However, not to include drama as a separate category is contrary to the way most arts curricula are conceived; I have therefore included fiction and drama as separate headings despite their close affinity. To repeat: the categories used here are a vehicle for discussing the issues and not recommendations for universal curriculum application.

Visual art

Visual art is sometimes referred to as 'art and design' or just 'art'. The distinction between 'art' and 'design' harks back to Collingwood's distinction between art and craft (1938: 15). He was concerned to disentangle the notion of craft from that of 'art proper' (ibid.: 15) on various grounds, including the fact that in the case of craft the process of planning has the end in sight right from the first stage of the project; a craft or design effort will result in a chair or bed-spread, whereas an artistic process is more open. The danger of this distinction is that it reinforces divisions between emotion and spontaneous expression on the one hand (art) and planning, form and technique (craft) on the other. The romantic view that the artist begins with a blank canvas and creates a work from inner feelings can lead to a very restricted approach to teaching the subject, as discussed in Chapter 3.

The tension between free expression and systematic instruction is found in the history of visual art. A key development was the recognition of child art as something distinct from adult art and to be valued in its own right. The influence of Rousseau placed an emphasis on natural development and this meant that self-expression through drawing and painting started to take precedence over mechanical copying. Spencer in 1878 declared that when the natural instinct of the child is allowed to emerge, 'the drawing of outlines immediately becomes secondary to colouring' (Macdonald, 1970: 321). Other factors which influenced the attention to child art were the increasing spread of developmental ideas in psychology, the recognition of so-called 'primitive' art as a sensitive form of expression, and the increasing appreciation of modern art. All these combined to challenge the traditional approach to teaching art; there was more emphasis on the need for the teacher to stimulate the imagination of the child, thus embodying a view of the artistic process contained in self-expression theories. There were also attempts to correct the inclination to take self-expression too far. The Norwood report wanted to see training in the necessary skills, because such training 'coordinates hand and eye and develops control' (Secondary School Examination Council, 1943: 126). The report, however, also recommended the development of a form of 'appreciation', the 'encouragement of the boys and girls to see with seeing eyes, to be aware of form and colour and design' (ibid.: 126). It was recommended that all children should have the opportunity of 'seeing the place of art in the spiritual and social and economic life of the present and the past. The study of a civilisation or an age can scarcely be undertaken without reference to its art' (ibid.: 127). Thus a more complete conception of the subject including making, responding, appreciating and contextualisation was already in evidence.

As with the other art forms, then, debates within visual art education reflected tensions between child- and subject-centred approaches, between self-expression and teaching of technique and between advocates of education in art and education through art (Hickman, 2005). A more complete conception of the subject recognises it not just as a focus for the development of individual creativity and imagination, or as a form of instruction in skills but also as a form of visual education or visual literacy, as cultural learning. Advocates of visual art (and the arts in general) often identify its value in relation to general aptitudes and key skills such as the development of creativity, problem-solving ability, physical dexterity and cognitive skills. These are important but the more distinct value of visual art is precisely its emphasis on the *visual*.

Jewitt (2008: 6) draws attention to the importance of the visual in everyday life in the twenty-first century which is 'saturated with image, visual technologies and visual practices'. This means that while recognising that visual art education has importance both historically and as a form of human expression it also needs to be seen as a form of visual education *per se*. This more inclusive view suggests a broad conception of the subject that erodes distinctions between 'art' and 'craft' or 'design'. Some writers have identified dangers in such a broad approach, that its outcomes become more utilitarian and functional, with less focus on the aesthetic.

> *Art education* thus becomes *visual education* and while it *is* seen as a way knowing, the particular kind of knowledge is often seen as being *more transactional than aesthetic* in nature. Learning about design has more to do with the outer objective world than the inner and personal world. Such an approach must stress the utilitarian rather than the symbolic, the functional rather than the aesthetic, the objective rather than the personal.
>
> (Morris, 1987: 199)

It is important to take note of these concerns but they are not necessarily resolved by creating a narrow art curriculum. Instead it is important to recognise the importance of understanding by curriculum developers, teachers and pupils. For it is *how* the subject is taught as much as *what* is taught that is important. There is no reason therefore for the art curriculum not to embrace elements such as architecture, photography and sculpture. This can happen without fear of a reductive, functional approach as long the important processes are understood. For example, in the case of architecture, Lyas (1997: 218) has pointed out 'the intended practical end for the building (and more generally, the intended end of a designed object, a teapot, say) is part of what has to be forged into the aesthetic end product'.

Fiction

The importance of story in people's lives seems so obvious it hardly seems worth stating. So many theorists do not bother, focusing instead on structure and forms of narratives or exploring the ways in which perspectives drawn from psychoanalysis, Marxism and post-colonialism can expand thinking and challenge naïve readings of texts. Such insights have value but sometimes obscure a more basic understanding of the role of fiction in our lives. In order to do so, it is helpful to distinguish narrative from fiction in that the former concept sometimes includes non-fiction accounts such as biographies, travelogues or blogs which may take a narrative form. Fiction on the other, like all art, operates in the realm of the 'unreal' and that is part of its power. It is also helpful to distinguish 'literature' from 'fiction' in that the latter concept includes certain types of television and film, though not all examples of both genres. By definition, fiction excludes documentaries, reality shows and other factual programmes. It is important to be aware of these differences but not to be obsessed by them. Some works play with the overlap between fiction and reality. The TV series *The Trip* with Coogan and Brydon was a clever satire of reality shows precisely because of this subtle ambiguity.

Armstrong's (2005) comments about the importance and origins of myth can apply more generally to the role of fictional narrative in human life. She points out that human beings are meaning-seeking creatures:

> [F]rom the very beginning we invented stories that enabled us to place our lives in a larger setting, that revealed an underlying pattern, and gave us a sense that, against all the depressing and chaotic evidence to the contrary, life had meaning and value.
>
> (Ibid.: 2)

She goes on to say that it is a peculiar characteristic of the human mind that we have imagination, the ability to think of something that is not immediately present or does not exist. Mythology (and fiction) therefore is not about opting out of the world but enabling us to live more intensely within it (ibid.: 3): 'Like a novel, an opera or a ballet, myth is make-believe; it is a game that transfigures our fragmented, tragic world, and helps us to glimpse new possibilities by asking "what if?"' (ibid.: 8).

This does not mean that there is consensus amongst writers about how art and fiction relate to our lives, especially moral lives. For several decades literary theorists have challenged the traditional humanist view that simple exposure to literature and the humanities makes us better human beings and helps us understand the human condition (Klages, 2006: 10). Literary and cultural theory has done much to revitalise the way we read texts, going beyond surface meanings to explore representations of gender, class and ideology. Reader-oriented theories in particular have had an important role to play in pedagogy, in drawing attention to the way the reader contributes to the meaning of the text. Literary theorists have also helped us recognise that reading of texts changes over time – that in reading or teaching fiction we are not in pursuit of one 'correct' reading. However, such insights should not detract from the important link between fiction and our moral lives.

In order to properly understand the relationship between fiction and morality, it is important to distinguish the concept of 'moral' from 'moralism', an idea that was introduced in Chapter 1 (Eagleton, 2003: 143). The latter concept is more about establishing rules and guidelines by seeking to draw out the key message of a work. It is a form of separatism in that it abstracts the idea from its context. It also seeks to separate content and form and reduces the fiction from a layered form of art to a transparent vehicle for conveying specific rules and obligations. The 'moral' in fiction works differently. It is more about exploring the texture and quality of human behaviour. A key moral dimension of Miller's play *All My Sons* is that instead of condemning Keller, the main protagonist, it reveals a more complex moral situation at work in terms of the protagonist's main motivation. He committed the crime of releasing faulty aeroplane parts out of loyalty to his son and family. Lamarque and Olsen (2004a: 202) argue that an adequate conceptual framework for describing the apprehension of a literary work needs the concept of 'enjoyment' as well as such concepts as 'meaning', 'understanding' and 'interpretation'. This is reminiscent of Shusterman's (2003) case for restoring a concept of 'entertainment' as discussed in Chapter 2. Concepts of enjoyment and entertainment interpreted in a deep rather than superficial sense further strengthen the general links between fiction and morality in that morality is 'the abundance of life' (Eagleton, 2003: 141).

Drama

The development of drama education is of particular interest because the differences of opinion have been well-defined and embody a number of the tensions that are found in art education more generally. Its association with the 'new education' movement meant that its early justification was in terms of individual personal growth and self-expression. It embodied ideas of natural development, child-centred education and experiential learning. The close affinity of 'drama' with 'play' seen in the young child's natural inclination to engage in spontaneous, dramatic playing meant that 'drama' from the 1950s onwards was often seen as something distinct from 'theatre'. The distinction was most notably captured by Way (1967: 2): '[T]heatre is largely concerned with communication between actors and an audience; "drama" is largely concerned with experience by the participants'. The strong divisions, which were at their most apparent in the 1970s and early 1980s, have given way in contemporary practice to a more inclusive approach to the subject where performance, improvisation, exercises and use of script all have their place. This comprehensive view of the subject is reflected both in the national curriculum and examination syllabuses in the UK and elsewhere. In retrospect it is tempting to see the rejection of theatre as just a strange aberration in drama's history that is best forgotten, but that view ignores the growth in thinking underlying those developments.

Just as we can only properly understand the growth of progressive ideas in education by seeing them not just in hindsight but in relation to what came before, we need some insight into the prevailing practice at the time in order to appreciate the intention and value of the reform movements in drama. The way in which the subject was conceived took a variety of forms, e.g. speech and elocution exercises, acting out plays and short scripts, mime and movement, performance on the stage (Boas and Hayden, 1938; Alington, 1961). However, many of the practices were highly regimented and mechanical, despite attaching the word 'creative' to the activities. The emphasis on external action and appearances rather than exploration of the potential for learning and transformation started to be questioned.

It was not so much theatre *per se* that started to concern critics but what might be termed 'theatricality', with its associations with exhibitionism, staginess and artificiality. Warnings about such dangers are found throughout the drama education literature. Finlay-Johnson (1911) was concerned to do away with 'acting for display', a point she makes twice in her book (Bolton, 1998: 16). Slade (1954: 351), in a memorable phrase, thought that pupils might be turned into 'bombastic little boasters' by going on stage. Allen (1979: 128) wrote about the standard school nativity play in which the pupils could not be heard and were more concerned with waving to the audience than attending to what they were doing. O'Neill and Lambert (1982: 25) thought that theatre could result in a 'superficial playing out of events, lacking in seriousness and sometimes accompanied by a degree of showing off'. Such criticisms are less often found in contemporary literature: no one wants to come across as a spoilsport or an outdated eccentric. It is widely acknowledged that young people can gain huge amounts at many levels from involvement in performances of different kinds. Yet many teachers who have been involved in school productions will recognise the potential dangers in becoming so focused on product and production values that the educational benefits are lost. The evidence of reality TV shows and of child stars that implode in later life indicates that the potential negative impact of exposure to public gaze needs to be taken seriously.

It was not just the dangers of premature performance that was questioned but also the stifling of creativity and self-expression along with the neglect of feeling. Slade (1954) influenced by developments in visual art education recognised child drama as a separate art form as opposed to adult theatre. Contrary to the way he is sometimes portrayed he was not anti-theatre but saw theatre as the culmination of a development process and was more appropriate for the young adult and less so for young children. His approach, which had strong echoes of Rousseau's romantic belief in natural development, was characterised by respect for the creative ability of children. He recommended minimum intervention by the teacher who was there to guide and nurture rather than instruct.

The work of Bolton and Heathcote in the 1970s brought a change of emphasis, although their work is often wrongly placed in the same 'self-expression' category. In their drama work more attention was paid to content. For example a play based on the Pied Piper would not just ask the pupils to mime the role of rats happily dancing along to the piper's music but would explore themes of trust and betrayal (Fleming, 2011a). The nature of the experience of the pupils and the role of the teacher in elevating the quality of the drama were key concerns. A lesson in the 1950s or early 1960s on the theme of a visit to the seaside might have involved the children performing actions to the teacher's commentary: 'One morning you wake up early and go into the bathroom to wash …' or else engaging in their own dramatic play by getting into an imaginary car, driving to the seaside and jumping in the sea. A Heathcote/Bolton approach, however, would seek to add depth and challenge the pupils' thinking and problem solving skills: for example, a drama about a trip to the seaside might become, under the teacher's influence, an examination of family expectations and the exercise of authority. Thus understanding and cognition were restored in drama work which had become more preoccupied with feeling (Fleming, 2010).

The development of thinking in drama education saw a gradual blending of the elements from the child-centred, play-oriented progressive tradition and the more positive elements from the theatre tradition. From the latter came elements of form, structure, technique, focus and control that were often missing from approaches that focused entirely on spontaneous improvisation or dramatic playing. At its best the progressive tradition injected dynamism, ownership, genuine growth and attention to process, which had been missing from purely product-oriented, mechanical practices. The best contemporary practice embraces theatre and performance as well as more process-orientated activities.

Although drama can in some ways be seen as a form of 'fiction' its unique value lies in its creation of a different kind of illusion concerned with the 'here and now' (Esslin, 1987: 3). It is above all a concrete activity that manifests in action, unlike the novel. It creates an 'eternal present' (ibid.: 25). Its power in part derives from the fact that it operates in real time and space with 'real' characters, unlike film, which Langer (1953: 412) astutely observes operates in a 'dream mode'. She does not mean that film copies dreams or puts us into a daydream but that it is projected to compose a 'finished experiential form' (ibid.: 412). Drama, on the other hand, presents a concrete, visible presence happening before us. The live element therefore is central to the nature and power of drama. It is of course precisely the power of this form that makes it a focus for learning in other subjects. This is entirely appropriate as long as this does not detract from the important entitlement of young people to be educated to practice, appreciate and understand this unique art form.

Music

Pater's (1986: 86) remark that all art 'constantly aspires towards the condition of music' is often quoted with approval but not always explained. One interpretation of what he meant is that with music there is little possibility of neglecting form because it is so central to the experience; 'it is perceived *entirely* and *only* through its own, tonally moving forms' and aspires to 'aesthetic self-sufficiency' (Herzog, 1996: 130). As discussed above, when teaching fiction it is possible to devalue the aesthetic experience by focusing only on the content in a way that is hardly possible with music. According to Graham (2000: 91), the unique claim for music is 'in providing us with extended structures of organised sound by means of which we may explore human experience and in conventional musical sound this richness is increased by the possibility on interpretative performance'. Swanwick (1999: 3) similarly refers to the way music 'significantly enhances and enriches our understanding of ourselves and the world' and 'has the power to lift us out of the ordinary, to elevate our experience beyond the everyday and the commonplace'. Moreover, the popularity of music in almost everyone's life, particularly amongst the young, is unquestionable. In 1963, the Newsom report commented on the contrast between the enthusiasm for music shown by young people who 'crowd into record shops' and the reality of the curriculum as experienced in schools (Central Advisory Council for Education, 1963). Despite its wide popularity, music has traditionally fared less well in formal education than the other arts. In the UK it has been for some years the arts subject that has the lowest take-up at GCSE level (Little, 2009). Plummeridge (2001: 21) has pointed out that 'music educationists often appear to be on the defensive' and the theme of music's low status often appears in writing about the subject.

As Cox (1997) rightly points out, learning in the arts takes place in informal as well as formal settings. Music has tended to succeed better in extra-curricular activities than in the normal curriculum. In school contexts it has sometimes been seen as a subject with elitist tendencies favouring the talented and excluding the majority. Its widespread popularity in wider society is not always accompanied by deep-seated appreciation of its value. All of the arts have suffered in an educational climate which prioritises value for money, observable outcomes, concrete objectives and accountability. But music does so perhaps more than the others. Despite some attempts to justify music on the basis of extrinsic justification, it needs to be seen primarily as an aesthetic subject with the key aim of contributing to a rich and fulfilled life. It can, however, be taken for granted with a failure to grasp specifically why the *teaching* of music is important. After all, most people have a natural affinity with the enjoyment of music, so why the need to include it as a subject in the curriculum? One answer is reflected in the notion of enrichment. While not denying the value of surface enjoyment and sensuous pleasure, education can enhance the potential for broader and deeper appreciation and understanding. The notion of breadth includes exposure to a wider range of forms and genres, including those from different cultures. The idea of depth includes understanding of technical issues, acquisition of skills and understanding cultural and historical contexts.

The history of music education has not shared all of the preoccupations of the other art subjects. For example, it has not come under quite as much influence from self-expression theorists as drama, although some tension between traditional and progressive approaches has been evident. A traditional approach tended to see music as a body of knowledge with the emphasis on appreciation and performance (which included singing). Progressives saw music in more expressive terms and thought children should be engaged in making music and experimenting with it themselves.

The social context has inevitably influenced attitudes to music education. In Victorian England there was a tendency to see music and art as upper-class hobbies for ladies. In elementary schools, the subject was more or less synonymous with singing; musical instruments were largely beyond the reach of the poor and economic factors are still relevant. The songs were often religious or patriotic and were often chosen for their moral content and contribution to national identity (Johnson, 1989). Musical appreciation was predominant in the 1920s and 1930s. The Hadow report (Board of Education, 1926: 238) specifically stated that the aim of music teaching considered as part of a school curriculum 'should be rather the cultivation of a taste than the acquirement of a proficiency; it should lay the foundation for intelligent study and enjoyment of music in after life'. The report went on to endorse the importance of the technical aspect of music but suggested that it should be 'subordinated to the human delight in beautiful sound, which is the basis and foundation of all music' (ibid.: 242).

By 1943 the Norwood report took a more balanced view between appreciation and what it termed 'executive skill', recommending that it is part of the teacher's work to cater for both. The benefits of music education are expressed predominantly in social terms.

> Membership of a choir or an orchestra gives valuable experience of coordinated effort and achievement; the individual has to subordinate himself to the collective purpose of the whole, which nonetheless depends upon him; children who are unable to take part in other cooperative activities often gain self-confidence and a sense of community from singing or taking part in an orchestra alongside their school-fellows.
>
> (Secondary School Examination Council, 1943: 126)

By 1967 the Plowden report was still commenting unfavourably on the state of music education in primary schools, referring to the 'unsatisfactory position' which would 'need to be tackled systematically and resolutely' (Central Advisory Council for Education, 1967: 252). The report expressed concern about the musical training received by teachers, which appears as another ongoing theme in much writing about primary music.

Notwithstanding the dangers of assuming a linear development of the subject, a broad, perhaps oversimplified, view of developments shows an increasing emphasis on musical appreciation in the early twentieth century, a greater focus on performance in the 1950s and more concern with improvising and composing in the 1970s. Pitts (2000: 204) has commented on

> a gradual shift in the views and methods of music educators in the twentieth century, broadly demonstrating an increasing acceptance of a wider musical repertoire, and a similar recognition of the variety of musical opportunities that can be made available to children.

Dance

Of all the art forms in education, dance is one which perhaps has received least attention and been most marginalised. There are reasons to explain its neglect as well as strong arguments to support its unique contribution and claim to be part of arts education. Shusterman (2006) has coined the term 'somaesthetics' to refer to an interdisciplinary research field that seeks to understand and advocate the importance of the body in human life. The neglect of the body is partly because the life of the mind has commanded so much attention in philosophy and, by extension, education. Much writing on arts in education has focused on the polarity between feeling and rationality with much less attention to an equally important mind/body dichotomy which has been prevalent. Somaesthetics, therefore, concerns the body 'as a locus of sensory aesthetic appreciation (*aisthesis*) and creative self-fashioning' (ibid.: 2). Shusterman points out that bodily training for wisdom and virtue has received more attention in Asian traditions, where it has been a dimension of ritual and artistic practices aimed at instilling mind/body harmony (ibid.: 17). There is potential for addressing issues related to the body in various parts of the curriculum notably the sciences, physical education and personal and social education, but dance has a special role to play.

In the UK, for many years dance has been found within the physical education rather than arts curriculum. This understandably has caused concern to the education dance community, but the related issues are not clear-cut. We may take the view as the OfSTED publication *The Arts Inspected* (1998) that how the subject is taught is more important than its place in the curriculum. However, the placing of dance can very easily influence the way it is conceptualised and taught. To say that placing the subject within physical education demeans dance is to provide an unjustifiably reductive view of sports. Sanderson (1996: 54) is one of the writers who has argued that dance has many genuine links with sport activities. After all, education in sport can make a claim to including the aesthetic as part of its goals and outcomes. Reid (1997: 13) comments that most writers agree that important aspects of physical education 'fall unequivocally within the area of the aesthetic' and others 'can at least be considered from the aesthetic view point'.

Conversely, there seems little point in excluding health and fitness objectives as part of the dance curriculum even though these are only one aspect of what it seeks to achieve. A helpful distinction here is between 'art' and the 'aesthetic' discussed in Chapter 2. It is the integrity of dance specifically as an art form that is important. This means that meaning, communication, intention and human expression are all central to the experience of dance.

Paradoxically, it is dance's power that can make it difficult to justify in discursive, propositional terms. Once we extend beyond matters of fitness and entertainment the language of justification can appear obscure and quasi-mystical, although once we are persuaded to see things in that way, the ideas are compelling. Langer (1953: 190) refers to dance in antiquity as 'the first presentation of the world as a realm of mystic forces' and claims 'it is the envisagement of a world beyond the spot and the moment of one's animal existence'. She goes on to say that dance 'creates the image of that pulsating organic life which formerly it was expected to give and sustain' (ibid.: 207). Like music, dance is less easily explained in functional terms. Although it does have some utility, its deep significance lies in its symbolic expression captured in the painting *Dance*, which depicts 'human solidarity and abandonment': 'Not only does Matisse's work present an authentic human involvement with others and the natural world; it somehow draws us into the dancers' movement and suggests the vital networks in which we live or ought to live our lives' (Greene, 1995: 62).

It is perhaps little wonder, then, that dance has not been given sufficient recognition in education. According to Haynes (1987: 142) there has been much less written about dance and much less tradition of scholarly research than is the case with the other forms. It is the more functional aspects of dance that have been emphasised in historical policy documents in the UK. In the nineteenth and early twentieth century, where it existed in schools, it was largely accepted for its physical and social rather than aesthetic benefits (Brook, 1989: 64). In the elementary school it was part of music and drill. Folk dance was the activity most widely recommended.

A new concept of dance placing more emphasis on spontaneous expression and 'natural' movement was pioneered by Isadora Duncan. There is much in common between her commitment to self-expression and her contemporary advocates of progressive education. She did not reject the development of technique but did not want the acquisition of skill to be seen as an end in itself. The Plowden report (Central Advisory Council for Education, 1967) acknowledged the teaching and writing of Laban as being a key influence on developments in the 1950s and 1960s. He also placed a strong emphasis on personal expression, spontaneous improvisation and experimentation, and saw creative activity as a means of evolving a style of dance which was 'true' to the individual personality (Haynes, 1987: 149).

Inevitably, divisions and differences of opinion grew in the field. Some writers and practitioners in education objected to the loss of dance technique with the emphasis on personal development (Taylor and Andrews, 1993: 34). A number of writers argued that dance education should change its emphasis from its more psychological/therapeutic orientation towards the more formal and aesthetic conception of dance as an art form. This development was further encouraged by the presence in England of the contemporary dance style of Martha Graham. There was a tendency for dance teachers to divide into opposing groups, a factor which has strong parallels with divisions in the drama world. One emphasised product, technique and performance, the other placed more emphasis on process, expression of feeling and individual development.

Contemporary curriculum documents are more balanced. At the time of writing dance in the UK still occurs within the PE programmes of study but makes reference to 'exploring and communicating ideas, concepts and emotions in relation to how well a performer or choreographer expresses ideas, feeling, concepts of emotions to communicate artistic or choreographic intention to an audience' (QCDA, 2011). The dance component of the Australian draft arts curriculum embraces the development of dance skills, knowledge and aesthetic learning; composing and performing; informed critical appreciation. It also makes reference to knowledge of styles including traditional and contemporary Aboriginal and Torres Strait Islander and Asian dance, and other Australian and international forms (ACARA, 2011).

Poetry

Our earliest experiences of language as children are more poetic than prosaic. Children delight in sounds, texture, images and rhythms without being obsessed by discursive meaning. As Preen (1999) has pointed out, children do not ask, in response to Humpty Dumpty, why on a wall not on a fence? On this basis the naturalistic account of art discussed in Chapter 2 applies to poetry in that its origins can be said to lie in the child's first encounter with the spoken word when the distinction between poetry and music is not clear-cut. In most school curricula, poetry is found with the language as subject curriculum where its integrity as an art form has often been distorted when it has been employed in a narrow way as a vehicle to teach language skill rather than as a genre to be enjoyed in its own right.

Consideration of how poetry has and is sometimes taught provides insight into the teaching of all of the art forms. There are of course no strict, universal rules with regard to teaching – depending on the circumstances there may be times when a particular approach is entirely appropriate. Nevertheless, it may be helpful to consider the types of approaches that are unhelpful if they dominate the classroom. In the following examples, poetry might be substituted by painting, sculpture, music composition etc.

A traditional approach to poetry involved the teacher leading the student through an inductive question-and-answer process to the 'correct' interpretation and analysis. This often meant the pupils' trying to guess what was in the teacher's head. 'What does the image of the moon mean?' 'No, think of x'. Pupils often experienced the poem in a disconnected, atomised way with no overall sense of its import or meaning. The teacher's role was to conduct the reading of the poem, and hope somehow that his or her reading would be appropriated by the pupils (Dias and Hayhoe, 1988: 7).

This inductive method came under criticism in some of the literature in the 1970s and 1980s but was in some classrooms replaced by another extreme, the independent group discussion. Here a poem was handed out in groups to the class for them to discuss without teacher intervention. On the face of it this seems suitably enlightened and appropriately influenced by reader-response theory, where the meaning of the poem arises through interaction between reader and text. The problem with the approach is that groups were often left floundering with obscure poems, either completely grasping the wrong end of the stick or getting frustrated.

Both of these teaching methods can suffer from a third type of poetry teaching which induces the pupils to see the poem as a puzzle to which the teacher or someone else has the key. Much modern poetry is deliberately ambiguous and invites the reader to speculate about meaning but to see such poems as having one 'solution' is to miss the point. Of course some poems are clearer and more accessible, but to see such works as puzzles is equally misguided. Langer (1953: 208) has pointed out the folly of constantly asking 'what the poet is trying to say' and to judge 'how well he says it'. For, 'if the reader can make clear what the poet is trying to say, why cannot the poet say it clearly in the first place?'. Klages (2006: 7) describes the way as a teacher she still asks 'why is this word here?' but is more concerned to answer 'what does it do, how does it function, what does it produce' than 'what does it mean?'.

A central challenge in teaching poetry is to maintain a balance between reader and text so that both are attended to. The same tension is present in approaches to writing poetry. In the belief that creativity (interpreted largely as originality) should be respected, pupils were often told to 'write a poem' with little or no further guidance or direction. The implicit romantic view was of poetry as a 'spontaneous overflow of powerful feelings' or that genuine poetry is 'composed in the soul'; the emphasis was primarily on the expression of private emotion. There was correspondingly an insufficient emphasis on the craft of writing, on the drafting process, and on a sheer delight in language. There is some danger that emphasis on form without sufficient motivation and engagement will promote mechanistic writing devoid of any real sense of meaning or purpose; all teachers will be familiar with the contorted meanings which some pupils produce in the pursuit of a rhyme. However, working with particular formal constraints can be very liberating and expressive (Fleming and Stevens, 2010: 172).

This chapter has focused on the separate art subjects in order to demonstrate the folly of simply lumping them all together and assuming that experience of one can stand for all. In practice, however, much innovative arts teaching works through integration. This is to be encouraged because the art forms themselves are not always discrete, as illustrated in the case of opera and musical theatre. Many of Hogarth's works can be seen as narratives, with *A Rake's Progress* taking the form of eight related paintings depicting a narrative sequence. New York artist John Spinks (2011) uses letters sent to him by his father from the North-East of England to create mixed media collages/paintings. Sections of the letters can still be read on the paintings but not in their entirety. Some of the content is appropriately sacrificed to the form and the beauty of the final product. The works are deeply personal and extol the art of letter writing (which is being lost in contemporary society) but in the transformation to art transcend the subjective and personal and have more universal significance. There is a strong element of social history both in the content of the letters and in the way they have been used. The works celebrate the value of the written word but also show its limitations by creating new meanings with added resonance and aesthetic power.

Further reading

For histories of the different art subjects see Bolton (1998) *Acting in Classroom Drama: A Critical Analysis*; Lewicki (1996) *From 'Play Way' to 'Dramatic Art'*; Macdonald (1970) *The History and Philosophy of Art Education*; Sutton (1967) *Artisan or Artist? A History of the Teaching of Arts and Crafts in English Schools*; Efland (1989) *A History of Art Education*; Cox (1993) *A History of Music Education in England 1872–1928*; Pitts (2000) *A Century of Change in Music Education: Historical Perspectives on Contemporary Practice*. There are a range of subject specific journals including: *Research in Drama Education*; *Research in Dance Education*; *Journal of Dance Education*; *The International Journal of Art and Design Education*; *Art Education Journal*; *International Journal of Education through Art*; *International Journal of Education and the Arts*; *Art Education Journal*; *British Journal of Music Education*; *International Journal of Music Education*; *Journal of Research in Music Education*; *English in Education*; *Use of English*.

10

Conclusion: the arts, culture and education

In the Introduction to this book two broadly different uses of 'understanding' were described. One sees the concept more as a single event, in the sense of coming to perceive something clearly. The other sees understanding more as a process of refining and deepening, making connections and seeing things in new ways. The terms 'analytic' and 'synthetic', which were used as a shorthand way of referring to these different types of emphasis, have been relevant to a number of the discussions in subsequent chapters in this book. The challenge of justifying the arts in education can be attempted in a rational, analytic way by listing reasons for teaching the arts. Alternatively, a holistic vision that attempts to show links between art and life in a more foundational way may offer a perspective that is missing from the more discursive formulation. The search for necessary and sufficient criteria for defining precisely what art is, has, in the past, given way in art theory to a less precise formulation. This is more in keeping with the way language has meaning. Classic distinctions between science and art, often conceived as analytic and synthetic approaches, were addressed in Chapter 4. It is more appropriate to speak of the 'histories' rather than the 'history' of art and art education, a view which is compatible with understanding as refining and deepening rather than seeing things unambiguously. The chapter on assessment put agreement in judgement rather than technical precision at the heart of the process, without underestimating the value of constantly seeking ways of making judgements more reliable.

When the two senses of 'understanding' are expanded in this way to embrace wider perspectives, what begins to emerge is not just two uses of a word but something more like two ways of being in the world. This is precisely the thesis of McGilchrist's monumental book *The Master and His Emissary* where he demonstrates that 'for us as human beings there are two fundamentally opposed realities, two different modes of experience' (McGilchrist, 2009: 3). In one we experience 'the live, complex, embodied, world'; in the other we give the kind of attention that 'isolates, fixes, and makes each thing explicit' (ibid.: 31). One approach is more logical, precise, restricted and mechanical; the other is more open, fluid and tolerant of ambiguities. In one (synthetic) case we

> allow things to be *present* to us in all their embodied particularity, with all their changeability and impermanence, and their interconnectedness, as part of a whole which is forever in flux. In this world we, too, feel connected to what we experience, part

of that whole, not confined in subjective isolation from a world that is viewed as objective.

(Ibid.: 93)

In the other (analytic) case we

step outside the flow of experience and 'experience' our experience in a special way: to *re-present* the world in a form that is less truthful, but apparently clearer, and therefore cast in a form which is more useful for manipulation of the world and one another. This world is explicit, abstracted, compartmentalised, fragmented, static (though its bits can be set in motion like a machine) essentially lifeless.

(Ibid.: 93)

Explaining the value of the arts in terms of different polarities is not unfamiliar to advocates and practitioners of the arts who often pit art against science, enlightenment thinking against romanticism, technical rationality against the richness of aesthetic engagement. However, employing these polarities in an oppositional way can lead to a weakness in the case made for the arts. For if we try to argue in favour of art *at the expense of* more explicitly rational ways of seeing the world that embrace science, logical thinking and evidence there will only ever be one winner. It is why arts advocacy can sometimes sound passionate but ultimately somewhat feeble and unconvincing. After all, mankind has always needed to eat, build shelters, develop forms of transport, and so on.

An equally common contemporary approach is not to pit one polar position against the other but to argue that such dichotomies are unhelpful and need to be transcended. However, this is equally misguided. Much writing in art and education has expressed its opposition to such binary divisions as that between feeling and cognition, reality and illusion, content and form, representation and expression, art and life. However, such constructs exist, and simply trying to put them aside by will is a bit like starting to give travel directions by saying, 'I wouldn't start from here'. The two ways of experiencing the world identified by McGilchrist should not be seen in opposition to each other but they also cannot just be ignored and dissolved. What is needed is an examination of how they relate to each other.

McGilchrist's thesis is that *both* ways of experiencing the world, which have their origins in the structure of the brain, are essential. He provides the memorable image of a bird who stays alive by using one eye to focus on pecking seed and the other for vigilant awareness of the environment (ibid.: 26). We need both narrow attention and broad contextual perception. His book is not a glorification of engaged feeling at the expense of detached thought, of integration at the expense of analysis. We do need to come to know the world in a way which is fixed, static, explicit, disembodied and general, for in that we way we advance new knowledge in many fields (ibid.: 131). However, we also need to have a vision of the world that is more holistic and integrated that does not see it just in a fragmented way. The book's title *The Master and His Emissary* comes from a story from Nietzsche about a ruler whose lands grew so large he needed to send emissaries as his representatives to look after the more distant regions. However, one of the emissaries thought he was wiser than his master and started to usurp his role; the domain eventually collapsed in tyranny. McGilchrist's view is that our civilisation has increasingly become dominated by one way of seeing the world that prioritises functionality, precision, categorical thinking, means–end rationality over vision and values. The emissary has become the master.

We do not have to look far in education to see convincing evidence to support this picture. In many societies education systems have become stifled by excessive bureaucracy, mechanical systems, quality control, quantitative judgements, clear outcomes and the pursuit of general rules that are oblivious to context. What we have witnessed in many countries has parallels with the colonisation of the 'lifeworld' by 'system' (Habermas, 1987). In the UK the introduction of the literacy strategy in the 1990s was well-meaning but deeply flawed because it was driven by the logical fantasy that quick-fix solutions could easily be found and put in place. It placed considerable emphasis on literacy attainment without understanding the need for literacy engagement (Guthrie, 2004). Some of the hastily produced materials (as well as being linguistically flawed) were based on very narrow thinking, structured to try to ensure progression and systematic coverage but with little recognition of the role played by learner motivation (Fleming, 2011a: 41). Similarly, the attempt to impose a uniform approach to planning and structuring lessons was highly misguided, yet driven by an inexorable logic that a centralised system devised by experts could be imposed successfully.

There has been a great deal of writing that has challenged a culture in education, dominant for so long in many countries, that puts testing before learning, accountability before growth, and rational planning before rich experience. Greene (1995: 2) felt convinced that people could 'choose to resist the thoughtlessness, banality, technical rationality … that now undermine public education at every turn'. However, challenges to contemporary practice can often come across as old-fashioned and airy-fairy, and vulnerable to the retort, 'surely you are not against assessment, lesson planning, inspection, accountability, discipline …', and so on. The value of McGilchrist's view is that we can recognise the importance of rationality, systems and logic as long as they are, so to speak, kept in their place. They need to be embedded in a broader vision that prioritises values, and respects what is implicit and contextual.

McGilchrist's book is in two parts. The first section focuses on the brain itself, examines its divided and asymmetrical nature and presents a large number of research studies that build a convincing picture of the importance of the two related ways of being in the world. What I have referred to as 'analytic' and 'synthetic' are associated with left and right hemispheres. The second half of the book examines the history of Western culture in the light of this analysis. With this historical perspective he illustrates his thesis that there has been a shift in the balance of power such that one way of being in the world which should have been servant has become master. His account is too rich to do justice to it in a simple summary. However, he associates the Renaissance with the dominance of the right hemisphere with the plays of Shakespeare a particular testimony to this fact:

> There is complete disregard for theory and for category, a celebration of multiplicity and the richness of human variety, rather than the rehearsal of common laws for personality and behaviour according to type. Shakespeare's characters are so stubbornly themselves, and not the thing that fate, or the dramatic plot, insist they should be,

that their individuality subverts the often stereotyped pattern of their literary and historical sources.

(Ibid.: 304)

In contemporary society precise, analytical thinking has taken precedence over contextual vision and experience so that an 'increasingly mechanistic, fragmented, decontextualised world has come about' (ibid.: 6). A more reasonable rather than rational approach to planning lessons and schemes of work would see a place for objectives and structures but would also recognise that learning should not be circumscribed by specifying outcomes and would recognise the need for flexibility and variety (Fleming, 2011a: 46).

Art derives from a vision that is integrated and contextual in which we connect with the world. The view that art provides an antidote to seeing the world in purely functional terms is also addressed by Shusterman (2002: 154) who argues that 'in a society dominated by ideals of material profit and means-end rationality, art's deep sense of play and non-instrumental purposiveness represents a striking and challenging alternative'. O'Toole (2009: 6) also points out the fundamental connections between play and art and that 'play and art are serious business'. This does not mean that we have to avoid any talk at all about the more specific functions of art in education, nor do we have to subscribe to a separatist, disinterested, purely intrinsic justification. As Shusterman says, 'Play does not entail art's failure to serve important social functions. Indeed, one valuable social function is to be an implicit critique of society's relentless functionalism' (ibid.: 154). Both a synthetic and an analytic approach also apply to the process of creating art. The holistic, integrated vision needs the complementary more static approach to unpack experience; art needs an element of distance and structure without which there would be no art only experience (ibid.: 199). In *The Birth of Tragedy*, Nietzsche defined two competing but complementary impulses in Greek culture – the Apollonian and Dionysian – that have parallels with these differences:

The Apollonian takes its name from Apollo, the god of flight, dream, and prophecy, while the Dionysian takes its name from Dionysus, the god of intoxication . . ... Apollo is associated with visible form, rational knowledge, and moderation, Dionysius with formless flux, mysticism and excess. The world of Apollo is made up of distinct moral individuals, while Dionysus presides over the dissolution of individual identity into a universal spiritual community uniting human beings with nature.

(Smith, 2000: xvi)

These distinctions and metaphors also have a direct application to pedagogy. We have seen how in the history of art education the role of the teacher was diminished under the influence of progressive ideas derived from Rousseau. The teacher became a kindly guide and facilitator of growth rather than someone who directly influenced the learning. Much educational writing of the last 60 years, through such concepts as scaffolding, conferencing, constructivism, active learning and formative assessment, has been trying to establish a more subtle conception of teaching that does not replace direct instruction with simply leaving students to their own devices. The concept of 'experiential learning' can easily be misunderstood as meaning just 'having experiences'; this was emphatically not what Dewey meant.

The title of Curtis's (1982) paper 'The True Secret of Education' comes from John Locke writing in 1690 who recognised the importance of knowing how to 'keep up a Child's Spirit, easy, active and free; and yet, at the same time, to restrain him from many things he has a mind to, and to draw him to things that are uneasy to him' (Locke, 1968). The learner needs to become *author* of his/her own thoughts and deeds; this is the mark of education and maturity. The true secret then is 'the secret of how we can push a child's spirit into such free activity in this continued and progressive enterprise of authorship' (Curtis, 1982: 516). This seems to be just a case of avoiding extremes but, according to Curtis, it is more than that, for it is the seeming contradiction that 'we must somehow by restraining and drawing him, get him to want for himself ' (ibid.: 517).

It is easy to sound reactionary when referring to the importance of the authority of the teacher (Furedi, 2009: 63). However, authority does not mean authoritarianism. Since the 1900s there have been many voices raised challenging the laissez-faire attitude to teaching and learning associated with extreme progressivism. However, the corrective attempt is often misplaced because it can so easily sound retrograde. This is where McGilchrist's analysis is helpful to pedagogy. The more synthetic, holistic approach recognises the need for the teacher to engage interest, make connections, relate what is new to previous experience, seek to motivate, provide a sense of the context, create enjoyment and excitement. But it is also important to go deeper, analysing effects, probing meanings, exploring interpretations, understanding references and allusions. This means more patient, painstaking application. As suggested in the Introduction to this book, teachers of the arts and other arts practitioners are invariably good at engaging students in exciting activities but not always as successful at ensuring focused learning, understanding and progression. This is understandable because, as has been argued, it is all too easy to fall into a process of arid analysis that is tedious and uninspiring. Teachers of other subjects are sometimes good at the detail but less successful at engaging interest; it is little wonder that there is an increasing effort to engage the arts in creative teaching and learning.

It has become something of a cliché to say that teaching itself is an art but some insight into the import of that claim can be seen when we recognise that good teaching requires subtle judgement and sensitivity to context, knowing when it is appropriate, for example, to engage, demonstrate, explain, exemplify, challenge, coax, direct, instruct or stay quiet. As with art, the best teaching has sufficient balance that absorbs the interest and subjectivity of the learner but is ultimately directed outwards to the object of learning/art product. It knows when it is appropriate to work at a surface level and when it is appropriate to push for greater depth.

This cycle from surface to depth analysis has parallels with Shusterman's (2002: 1) view of aesthetic experience that recognises that aesthetics stresses both 'surface and depth, impassioned immediacy of experience yet cool critical distance of judgment'. We may enjoy an aesthetic experience without going beyond immediate impressions, but interpretation can help us appreciate art:

> Aesthetics surely gains in knowledge the more it digs beneath the sensory surface, yet this metaphoric trajectory of ever-increasing depth presents a paradoxical image.

On our round earth, the deepest soundings should eventually bring us back to the surface again.

(Ibid.: 2)

This metaphor has valuable implications both for the teaching of art and for teaching in general. Shusterman's argument throughout the book is for greater recognition of the rich dialectical connection between surface and depth, and is a reminder that in the process of closer analysis there is a need to keep the wider context in mind and to retain intensity and immediacy of experience. It was probably recognition of this need that underpinned the attempt to impose compulsory 'plenary sessions' in lessons during the literacy strategy debacle in the UK. In its own ham-fisted way there was an element of perceptive insight underlying this policy – the mistake was to make it routine and formulaic.

That is why it is important at this point in this book to resist the temptation to create a diagram with boxes and arrows, and concepts of surface and depth, analysis and synthesis in order to show a 'model' of pedagogy. Such moves are fashionable in contemporary books about education but it would be misguided on two counts. First of all, it would be an attempt to pin down in a static, mechanised way something that should be resistant to rules and formulae. Second, it would create the illusion that something entirely new is being said here. That is not the case. What has been described is exactly what good teachers of all subjects, and particularly the arts, do. The aim here is to deepen understanding by making further connections and seeing things in new ways.

The resistance to rule-following can extend the parallels between teaching and art. Lyas (1997: 78) refers to the folly of 'importing into aesthetics the prestige of science'. By that he means the attempt to seek observable, universal rules that can determine the presence of aesthetic quality. Croce (1992: 123) called this kind of mistake the 'astrology of the aesthetic'. Tolstoy (1995: 50) was equally dismissive of the attempt to create a science of aesthetics and was critical of aesthetic theories. Wittgenstein (1969b: 18) refers to our 'craving for generality', which it can be seen emanates from an analytic way of seeing the world. Our ability to generalise and theorise is essential, for without it we would struggle to advance knowledge. However, the value of a more synthetic vision is that it attends to the limits of what is appropriate in terms of generalisation and theorising. Understanding requires intuitive sensitivity in specific contexts, not just generalised formulaic explanations. Wittgenstein's criticism of Frazer's *The Golden Bough* was because he thought its author over-generalised and misunderstood primitive rituals, interpreting them as scientific errors.

The fundamental reason why Wittgenstein condemns Frazer's explanations is not simply that they are false or at any rate highly contestable. It is simply that they are explanations, and that explanation serves to prevent us seeing what should really attract our attention.

(Bouveresse, 2008: 5)

Early theories that attempted to pin down the concept of 'art' in very precise ways now seem misguided. In contemporary society it is important to be aware of plurality and the dangers of excessive generalisation for moral as well as theoretical reasons.

The concept of interculturalism in education has been adopted by teachers of foreign languages to indicate that learning a language is not just a matter of learning a linguistic code but is also to some degree a matter of learning a culture. Language cannot be isolated from its sociocultural context. The term 'intercultural' has also been used by educators and trainers in the USA and Europe to refer to the preparation given to people who are planning a residence abroad for reasons to do with work or education. The assumption is that in order to come to terms with a different culture an appropriate form of induction is needed, often taking the form of acquiring knowledge and understanding of different customs and practices. At a deeper level, the acquisition of intercultural competence involves developing not just knowledge, skills but also attitudes and values (Byram, 1997). This involves being able to 'decentre', to be able to question what is often taken for granted in one's own culture. An intercultural attitude is about curiosity and openness to others and a willingness to relativise one's own values, beliefs and behaviours or to defamiliarise the familiar. An important element is to be able to see things in new ways, which the experience of art helps us to do so well.

The contrast between 'separatist' and 'inclusive 'concepts of art has informed several of the discussions in this book. One meaning of 'inclusive' is that it embraces art from a variety of cultures. As Leuthold (2011: 44) has said:

> To understand expressions from within the perspective of members of another culture is a form of Othering that creates the possibility of an expansive understanding of one's own. This involves an effort to transcend the limits inherent in stereotypical and touristic views of Others in favour of an empathetic engagement with difference.

There is an important role for art education in exploring work from a diversity of cultures but there is an even more basic sense in which art education itself can be seen as a form of decentring and widening of perspectives and extending understanding.

In providing a short summary of some of the key discussions in this book out of context there is a danger of distortion. However, given that understanding is promoted more by dialogue than through attempts at persuasion, it is hoped that the following summary will provoke the reader to further thoughts.

We need to retain the concepts of 'art' and 'arts in education' and resist any implicit inclination to see the concepts dissolve into notions of culture and creative learning. We do not need to employ a narrow, closed, fixed definition of 'art' to make it usable as a concept. It is important, however, to recognise the importance of human intentionality associated with the 'art space'. On this basis, it helps to distinguish the concept of 'art' from the 'aesthetic'. The latter concept is both narrower (when it refers to form) and broader (when it refers to sensuous appreciation). The concepts of beauty and the aesthetic are both important in education in all aspects of the curriculum, in, for example, notions of environmentalism and appreciating nature and landscapes. However, the concept of 'art' is more restricted because it is deliberately made by intentional human beings.

Justifying the arts in education by setting it up in *opposition to* logical, rational, technical, scientific ways of seeing the world is theoretically unsound and doomed to failure.

Such arguments explain why art is often undervalued. By linking art with humanity and our moral lives we are able to see it as foundational and basic. That does not mean that other advantages for teaching the arts are not worth exploring; it is helpful to distinguish between the specific *aims* of arts teaching and the *consequences or benefits* of the arts. Nor does it mean that employing art across the curriculum is not worthwhile as long as it does not erode the importance of specific subject teaching.

One meaning of the idea of an inclusive approach to arts education is to embrace a diversity of art forms and genres in the classroom. There is no justification for sustaining a division between high and low art; the gradations of quality are far more subtle. It is important to help pupils understand, appreciate and criticise all sorts of work. That does not mean jettisoning notions of great art; it can be argued that pupils have an entitlement to be introduced to what is generally considered the best. This term is not a static descriptor but is one which is subject to discussion and dialogue within communities of practice. Teachers of the arts are not forced to choose between either relativism or elitism.

One way of avoiding this dilemma is engage students themselves in meta-questions about art, the nature of art and how it functions in society. This needs to happen at an appropriate level of maturity, but the empirical data reported in Chapter 4 revealed that pupils age 12–13 years were ready to engage in such questions. This can also happen in the course of the students' own creation of art. A developmental perspective on arts education which was embraced by some of the progressive educators is helpful. It recognises that very young children are more likely to be engaged in making than responding to art made by others, but as young people mature, the sphere of reference needs to be broadened. The role of interpretation and criticism has often been undervalued in arts education theory and practice. An important part of acquiring artistic competence is for young people to understand how their own enjoyment of art can be enhanced by social and historical understanding, as well as through the opinions and interpretation of others. For example, they need to know when it is appropriate and when it is not to criticise a work by saying that aspects of it are 'unrealistic' or 'far-fetched'. This is not a matter of acquiring general rules but of gaining experience through exposure to a range of particular works and styles and being guided by sensitive teaching.

The consideration of social context and history when studying works of art may open up new possibilities of understanding. This is a very different conception from the traditional habit of providing anodyne background details on the artist's life, but rather includes a consideration of ideological context to challenge thinking. A separatist account of art still tends to dominate the consciousness of many art educators. However, in embracing a more inclusive account it also helps to recognise the powerful insights provided by the separatist view. It highlights the importance of notions of enjoyment seen in an appropriately deep way. It also acknowledges that art works in the realm of the 'unreal'. Paradoxically it is the separation from life's complexity and flux that provides understanding and insight. The very term 'the arts' can deceive us into making general claims that are unwarranted. It is worth recognising that different art forms and different works frequently have different intentions and effects. All of the different art subjects have a unique claim to a place on the curriculum.

Teaching art involves a subtle mix of such activities as setting tasks, demonstrating, explaining, providing background contextual information and making links. The rewards we get from art are not always instantaneous and may take time. Students may need to be helped to notice some things rather than others and have their attention directed to particular aspects of an art work. Teaching art is not just a matter of cold analysis of form but has to do with engaging pupils in creating their own work and formulating a dynamic response to art. It is important not to assume that the art object will, so to speak, induce a response by itself. Concepts of teacher leadership, direction and authority can sound reactionary but they need to be seen and interpreted positively and with discrimination. The key to achieving the appropriate balance in pedagogy is not following rules but developing *understanding*, an appropriate note on which to conclude.

Further reading

For discussion of the relationship between art and play see Schiller (2004), Adorno (1984) and Gadamer (2004). *The Continental Aesthetic Reader* edited by Cazeaux (2011) has an impressive collection of readings under the following headings: Nineteenth Century German Aesthetics; Phenomenology and Hermeneutics; Marxism and Critical Theory; Excess and Affect; Embodiment and Technology; Poststructuralism and Postmodernism; Aesthetic Ontologies. For an article on the importance of educating audiences see Young (2010). The book *Education in the Arts* edited by Sinclair *et al.* (2009) has a helpful chapter describing an integrated arts project in a primary school. The *Languages in Education, Languages for Education* platform of resources at the Council of Europe has many useful papers on pluralism, interculturalism and related issues (www.coe.int/t/dg4/linguistic/ langeduc/le_platformintro_EN.asp).

Bibliography

Abbs, P. (ed.) (1987) *Living Powers: The Arts in Education*. London: Falmer Press.

Abbs, P. (1989) *A Is for Aesthetic: Essays on Creative and Aesthetic Education*. London: Falmer Press.

Abbs, P. (1992) 'The Generic Community of the Arts: Its Historical Development', *Journal of Art and Design Education*, 11 (3), 265–286.

Abbs, P. (1994) *The Educational Imperative*. London: Falmer Press.

Abbs, P. (2003) *Against the Flow: Education, the Arts and Postmodern Culture*. London: RoutledgeFalmer.

Adorno, T. (1984) *Aesthetic Theory*. London: Routledge.

Aldrich, R. (ed.) (2002) *A Century of Education*. London: RoutledgeFalmer.

Alexander, H. (2006) 'A View from Somewhere: Explaining the Paradigms of Educational Research', *Journal of Philosophy of Education*, 40 (2), 205–221.

Alington, A. (1961) *Drama and Education*. Oxford: Basil Blackwell.

Allen, J. (1979) *Drama in Schools: Its Theory and Practice*. London: Heinemann.

Allen, R. and Turvey, M. (eds) (2001) *Wittgenstein, Theory and the Arts*. London: Routledge.

Armstrong, K. (2005) *A Short History of Myth*. Edinburgh: Canongate.

Arnold, M. (2006) *Culture and Anarchy*. Oxford: Oxford University Press. (First published 1869.)

Arts Council (2009) 'Artistic Assessment Scheme'. Online: www.artscouncil.org.uk/news/artistic-assessment-scheme/ (retrieved June 2011).

Arts Council (2010) *Achieving Great Art for Everyone: A Strategic Framework for the Arts*. London: Arts Council.

Atkinson, D. and Dash, P. (2005) *Social and Critical Practices in Art Education*. London: Trentham.

Audi, R. (ed.) (1999) *Cambridge Dictionary of Philosophy*, 2nd edition. Cambridge: Cambridge University Press.

Australian Curriculum, Assessment and Reporting Authority (ACARA) (2011) *Australian Curriculum*. Online: www.acara.edu.au (retrieved June 2011).

Bagley, C. and Cancienne, M. (2001) 'Educational Research and Intertextual Forms of (Re)Presentation: The Case for Dancing the Data', *Qualitative Enquiry*, 7 (2), 221–237.

Banaji, S., Burn, A. and Buckingham, D. (2010) *The Rhetorics of Creativity: A Review of the Literature*, 2nd edition. London: Creative Partnerships, Arts Council England.

Barone, T. and Eisner, E. (1997) 'Arts-Based Educational Research', in Jaeger, R. (ed.) *Complementary Methods for Research in Education*. Washington, DC: American Educational Research Association, 73–103.

Barone, T. and Eisner, E. (2011) *Arts Based Research*. London: Sage.

Batteux, A. (1997) 'The Fine Arts Reduced to a Single Principle', in Feagin, S. and Maynard, P. (eds) *Aesthetics*. Oxford: Oxford University Press, 102–104. (First published 1746 in French.)

Baugh, B. (2004) 'Prologemena to an Aesthetics of Rock Music', in Lamarque, P. and Olsen, S. (eds) *Aesthetics and the Philosophy of Art*. Oxford: Blackwell, 498–504.

Beardsley, M. (1966) *Aesthetics: From Classical Greece to the Present*. New York: Macmillan.

Bedford, E. (1956) 'Emotions', *Proceedings of the Aristotelian Society, 1956–57* (suppl.), 58, 281–303.

Bell, C. (1931) *Art*. London: Chatto & Windus. (First published 1913 by Richard Stokes.)

Bennett, T., Grossberg, L. and Morris, M. (2005) *New Keywords: A Revised Vocabulary of Culture and Society*. Oxford: Blackwell.

Berger, J. (1972) *Ways of Seeing*. London: Pelican.

Bermúdez, J. and Gardner, S. (eds) (2003) *Art and Morality*. London: Routledge.

Best, D. (1985) *Feeling and Reason in the Arts*. London: George Allen & Unwin.

Best, D. (1992) *The Rationality of Feeling*. London: Falmer Press.

Best, D. (1995) 'The Dangers of Generic Arts: Philosophical Confusions and Political Expediency', *Journal of Aesthetic Education*, 29 (2), 79–91.

Black, P. (1998) *Testing: Friend or Foe? Theory and Practice of Testing and Assessment*. London: Falmer Press.

Black, P., Harrison, C., Lee, C. and Marshall, B. (2003) *Assessment for Learning: Putting It Into Practice*. Maidenhead: Open University Press.

Blumenfeld-Jones, D. (1995) 'Dance as a Mode of Research Representation', *Qualitative Inquiry*, 1 (4), 391–401.

Board of Education (1923) *Differentiation of the Curriculum for Boys and Girls Respectively in Secondary Schools*. The Hadow Report. London: HMSO.

Board of Education (1926) *The Education of the Adolescent*. The Hadow Report. London: HMSO.

Board of Education (1931) *The Primary School*. The Hadow Report. London: HMSO.

Board of Education (1937) *Handbook of Suggestions for Teachers*. London: HMSO.

Board of Education (1938) *Report of the Consultative Committee on Secondary Education, with special reference to grammar schools and technical high schools*. The Spens Report. London: HMSO.

Board of Education (1959) *Primary Education*. London: HMSO.

Boas, G. and Hayden, H. (1938) *School Drama: Its Practice and Theory*. London: Methuen.

Boden, M. (ed.) (1996) *Dimensions of Creativity*. Cambridge, MA: MIT Press.

Bolton, G. (1984) *Drama as Education*. London: Longman.

Bolton, G. (1998) *Acting in Classroom Drama: A Critical Analysis*. Stoke on Trent: Trentham Books.

Boughton, D., Eisner, E. and Ligtovet, J. (1996) *Evaluating and Assessing the Visual Arts in Education*. New York: Columbia University.

Bourdieu, P. (1984) *Distinction: A Social Critique of Taste*. London: Routledge. (First published 1979 in French.)

Bouveresse, J. (2008) 'Wittgenstein's Critique of Frazer', in Preston, J. (ed.) *Wittgenstein and Reason*. Oxford: Blackwell, 1–20.

Bragg, S. (2007) *Consulting Young People*. London: Creative Partnerships, Arts Council England.

Brehony, K. (2001) 'From the Particular to the General, the Continuous to the Discontinuous: Progressive Education Revisited', *History of Education*, 30 (5), 413–432.

Bresler, L. (ed.) (2007) *International Handbook of Research in Arts Education*, Parts 1 and 2. Dordrecht: Springer.

Broadfoot, P. (1996) *Education, Assessment and Society*. Milton Keynes: Open University Press.

Brook, J. (1989) 'Modernism and the Expressivist Tradition in Dance in Education', in Ross, M. (ed.) *The Claims of Feeling: Readings in Aesthetic Education*. London: Falmer Press.

Broudy, H. (1991) 'The Arts as Basic Education', in Smith, R. and Simpson, A. (eds) *Aesthetic and Arts Education*. Chicago: University of Illinois Press, 125–133.

Bullough, E. (1912) 'Psychical Distance as a Factor in Art and an Aesthetic Principle', *British Journal of Psychology*, 5 (2), 87–118.

Burckhardt, J. (1929) *The Civilisation of the Renaissance in Italy*. London: George Harrap.

Burgin, V. (1986) *The End of Art Theory: Criticism and Postmodernity*. Basingstoke: Palgrave.

Byram, M. (1997) *Teaching and Assessing Intercultural Competence*. Clevedon: Multilingual Matters.

Cahnmann-Taylor, M. and Siegesmund, R. (eds) (2008) *Arts-Based Research in Education: Foundations for Practice*. London: Routledge.

Cannatella, H. (2008) *The Richness of Art Education*. Rotterdam: Sense Publishers.

Carey, J. (2005) *What Good Are the Arts?* London: Faber & Faber.

Carroll, N. (1998) *A Philosophy of Mass Art*. Oxford: Oxford University Press.

Cazeaux, C. (ed.) (2011) *The Continental Aesthetic Reader*. London: Routledge.

Central Advisory Council for Education (1963) *Half Our Future: The Newsom Report*. London: HMSO.

Central Advisory Council for Education (1967) *Children and their Primary Schools: The Plowden Report*. London: HMSO.

Central Advisory Council for England (1959) *The Crowther Report 15 to 18*. London: HMSO.

Charlton, W. (1970) *Aesthetics*. London: Hutchinson.

Clark, J. and Goode, T. (1999) (eds) *Assessing Drama*. London: National Drama Publication.

Clark, K. (1961) *Landscape Into Art*. London: Pelican.

Cohen, L., Manion, L. and Morrison, K. (2007) *Research Methods in Education*, 6th edition. London: Routledge.

Collingwood, R. (1938) *The Principles of Art*. Oxford: Clarendon Press.

Comerford Boyes, L. and Reid, I. (2005) 'What Are the Benefits for Pupils Participating in Arts Activities? The View from the Research Literature', *Research in Education–Manchester*, 73 (1), 1–14.

Cook, C. (1917) *The Play Way*. London: William Heinemann.

Cooper, D. (ed.) (1995) *A Companion to Aesthetics*. Oxford: Blackwell.

Coren, V. (2011) 'Be Prepared for No Boy Scouts', *The Observer*, 20 March.

Courtney, R. (1965) *Teaching Drama*. London: Cassell.

Cox, G. (1993) *A History of Music Education in England 1872–1928*. Aldershot: Scolar Press.

Cox, G. (1997) 'The Teaching and Learning of Music in the Settings of Family, Church and School: Some Historical Perspectives', in Bresler, L. (ed.) *International Handbook of Research in Arts Education*, Part 1. Dordrecht: Springer, 67–80.

Cox, S. (2000) 'Critical Enquiry in Art in the Primary School Critical Studies', *Art and Design Education*, 19 (1), 54–63.

Craft, A. (2006) 'Fostering Creativity with Wisdom', *Cambridge Journal of Education* 36 (3), 337–350.

Craft, A., Jeffrey, B. and Leibling, M. (eds) (2001) *Creativity in Education*. London: Continuum.

Crawford, D. (2001) 'Kant', in Gaut, B. and Lopes, D. (eds) *The Routledge Companion to Aesthetics*. London: Routledge.

Croce, B. (1992) *The Aesthetics as the Science of Expression and of the Linguistic in General*. Cambridge: Cambridge University Press.

Cropley, C. and Cropley, D. (2008) 'Resolving the Paradoxes of Creativity: An Extended Phase Model', *Cambridge Journal of Education*, 38 (3), 355–373.

Curtis, B. (1982) 'The True Secret of Education', *Philosophy* 57 (222), 515–528.

Curtis, S. and Boultwood, M. (1953) *A Short History of Educational Ideas*. London: University Tutorial Press.

Daldry, S. (1998) Preface to Hornbrook, D. (ed.) *On the Subject of Drama*. London: Routledge.

Danto, A. (1997) *After the End of Art: Contemporay Art and the Pale of History*. Princeton, NJ: Princeton University Press.

Danto, A. (2004) 'The Artworld', reprinted in Lamarque, P. and Olsen, S. (eds) *Aesthetics and the Philosophy of Art*. Oxford: Blackwell, 27–34. (First published 1964.)

Darling, J. and Nordenbo, S. (2003) 'Progressivism', in Blake, N., Smeyers, P., Smith, R. and Standish, P. (eds) *The Blackwell Guide to the Philosophy of Education*. Oxford: Blackwell.

Davies, S. (2004) 'Rock Versus Classical Music', in Lamarque, P. and Olsen, S. (eds) *Aesthetics and the Philosophy of Art*. Oxford: Blackwell, 505–516.

Davis, D. and Byron, K. (1988) 'Drama Under Fire – The Way Forward', *2D*, 8 (1), 26–27.

Deasy, R. (ed.) (2002) *Critical Links: Learning in the Arts and Student Academic and Social Development*. Washington, DC: Arts Education Partnership. Online: www.aep-arts.org.

Department for Education and Skills (2003) *Excellence and Enjoyment: A Strategy for Primary Schools*. London: DfES.

Department of Education and Science (1980) *A View of the Curriculum*. HMI Series: Matters for Discussion No. 11, London: HMSO.

Dewey, J. (2005) *Art as Experience*. New York: Penguin. (First published 1934.)

Dias, P. and Hayhoe, M. (1988) *Developing Response to Poetry*. Milton Keynes: Open University Press.

Dickens, C. (1989) *Hard Times*. Oxford: Oxford University Press. (First published 1854.)

Dickie, G. (1964) 'The Myth of the Aesthetic Attitude', *American Philosophical Quarterly*, 1 (1), 56–65.

Dickie, G. (1974) *Art and the Aesthetic*. Ithaca, NY: Cornell University Press.

Dickie, G. (1983) 'The New Institutional Theory of Art', *Proceedings of the 8th Wittgenstein Symposium*, Vol. 10, 57–64. (Reprinted in Lamarque, P. and Olsen, S. (eds) (2004) *Aesthetics and the Philosophy of Art*. Oxford: Blackwell, 47–54.)

Dissanayake, E. (2000) *Art and Intimacy: How the Arts Began*. Seattle: University of Washington Press.

Doddington, C. (2010) 'Mimesis and Experience Revisited' (review article), *Journal of Philosophy of Education*, 44 (4), 579–587.

Dorn, C. (1999) *Mind in Art: Cognitive Foundations in Art Education*. London: Routledge.

Dowling, L. (1988) 'Aestheticism', in Kelly, M. (ed.) *Encyclopedia of Aesthetics*. Oxford: Oxford University Press, 32–37.

Downing, D., Johnson, F. and Kaur, S. (2003) *Saving a Place For the Arts? A Survey of the Arts in Primary Schools in England*. Slough: NFER.

Dunn, J. (2008) 'Year of Paul 5: The Body of Christ', *The Pastoral Review*, December.

Eagleton, T. (1983) *Literary Theory: An Introduction*. Oxford: Basil Blackwell.

Eagleton, T. (1990) *The Ideology of the Aesthetic*. Oxford: Basil Blackwell.

Eagleton, T. (2003) *After Theory*. London: Allen Lane.

Eaton, M. (1988) *Basic Issues in Aesthetics*. Belmont, CA: Wadsworth.

Eaton, M. (2001) *Merit, Aesthetic and Ethical*. Oxford: Oxford University Press.

Edgeworth, M. and Edgeworth, R. L. (1855) *Practical Education*. New York: Harper and Brothers. (First published 1798.)

Efland, A. (1989) *A History of Art Education: Intellectual and Social Currents in Teaching the Visual Arts*. New York: Teachers' College Press.

Efland, A. (2002) *Art and Cognition: Integrating the Visual Arts in the Curriculum*. New York: Teachers' College Press.

Efland, A. (2004a) 'Eisner's *The Arts and the Creation of Mind*: Eisner's Contributions to the Arts in Education', *The Journal of Aesthetic Education*, 38 (4), 71–80.

Efland, A. (2004b) 'Art Education as Imaginative Cognition', in Eisner, E. and Day, M. (eds) *Handbook of Research and Policy in Arts Education*. Mahwah, NJ: Lawrence Erlbaum, 751–773.

Eisner, E. (1998) 'Does Experience in the Arts Boost Academic Achievement?', *Art Education*, 51 (1), 7–15.

Eisner, E. (2002) *The Arts and the Creation of Mind*. New Haven, CT: Yale University Press.

Eisner, E. and Day, M. (eds) (2004) *Handbook of Research and Policy in Art Education*. Mahwah, NJ: Lawrence Erlbaum.

Eliot, G. (1994) *Middlemarch*. London: Penguin. (First published as a serial 1871–1872.)

Elkins, J. (2002) *Stories of Art*. London: Routledge.

Elliott, R. (1972) 'Aesthetic Theory and the Experience of Art', reprinted in Osborne, H. (ed.) *Aesthetics*. Oxford: Oxford University Press, 145–157. (First published 1966.)

Elliott, R. (1991) 'Versions of Creativity', in Smith, R. and Simpson, A. (eds) *Aesthetics and Arts Education*. Chicago: University of Illinois Press, 60–71. (First published 1971.)

Esslin, M. (1987) *The Field of Drama*. London: Methuen.

Evans, R. (2011) 'The Wonderfulness of Us: The Tory Interpretation of History', *London Review of Books*, 17 March, 9–12.

Fairfield, P. (2009) *Education After Dewey*. London: Continuum.

Feagin, S. and Maynard, P. (1997) (eds) *Aesthetics*. Oxford: Oxford University Press.

Feyerabend, P. (1975) *Against Method: Outline of an Anarchistic Theory of Knowledge*. London: NLB.

Finch, H. (1995) *Wittgenstein*. Dorset: Element Books.

Fines, J. and Verrier, R. (1974) *The Drama of History*. London: New University Education.

Finlay-Johnson, H. (1911) *The Dramatic Method of Teaching*. London: Blackie.

Fisher, J. (2001) 'High Art Versus Low Art', in Gaut, B. and Lopes, D. (eds) *The Routledge Companion to Aesthetics*. London: Routledge, 409–421.

Fleming, M. (1992) 'Pupils' Perceptions of the Nature of Poetry', *Cambridge Journal of Education* 22 (1), 31–43.

Fleming, M. (2006a) *Evaluation and Assessment*. Strasbourg: Council of Europe.

Fleming, M. (2006b) 'Justifying the Arts: Drama and Intercultural Education', *Journal of Aesthetic Education* 40 (1), 54–64.

Fleming, M. (2009) 'The Challenge of Competence', in Hu, A. and Byram, M. (eds) *Interkulturelle Kompetenz und fremdsprachliches Lernen* [Intercultural Competence and Foreign Language Learning]. Tubingen: Gunter Narr Verlag.

Fleming, M. (2010) *Arts in Education and Creativity*, 2nd edition. London: Arts Council.

Fleming, M. (2011a) *Starting Drama Teaching*, 3rd edition. London: Routledge.

Fleming, M. (2011b) 'Learning in and Learning Through the Arts', in Sefton-Green, J., Thomson, P., Jones, K. and Bresler, L. (eds) *The Routledge International Handbook of Creative Learning*. London: Routledge.

Fleming, M. and Stevens, D. (2010) *English Teaching in the Secondary School: Linking Theory and Practice*, 3rd edition. London: Routledge.

Forge, The (2011) (Arts agency). Online: www.intheforge.com

Forrest, M. (2011) 'Justifying the Arts: The Value of Illuminating Failures', *Journal of Philosophy of Education*, 45 (1), 59–73.

Foster, H., Krauss, R., Bois, Y. and Buchloh, B. (2004) *Art Since 1900*. London: Thames & Hudson.

Foucault, M. (1989) *The Order of Things*. London: Routledge. (First published 1966 in French.)

Freeland, C. (2001) *But Is It Art?* Oxford: Oxford University Press.

Furedi, F. (2009) *Wasted: Why Education Isn't Educating*. London: Continuum.

Gadamer, H. (2004) *Truth and Method* (trans. J. Weinsheimer and D. Marshall), revised 2nd edition. London: Continuum.

Gallagher, K. (2007) 'Conceptions of Creativity in Drama in Education', in Bresler, L. (ed.) *International Handbook of Research in Arts Education*, Part 2. Dordrecht: Springer, 1229–1240.

Garner, R. (1990) 'Jacob Burckhardt as a Theorist of Modernity: Reading *The Civilisation of the Renaissance in Italy*', *Sociological Theory*, 8 (1), 48–57.

Gillard, D. (2004) 'The Plowden Report', *The Encyclopaedia of Informal Education*. Online: www.infed.org/schooling/plowden_report.htm (retrieved May 2011).

Gingell, J. (2000) 'Plato's Ghost: How Not to Justify the Arts', *Westminster Studies in Education*, 23 (1), 71–79.

Gingell, J. and Brandon, E. P. (2000) 'Special Issue: In Defence of High Culture', *Journal of Philosophy of Education*, 34 (3).

Gipps, C. (1994) *Beyond Testing*. London: Falmer Press.

Glock, H. (1996) *A Wittgenstein Dictionary*. Oxford: Blackwell.

Gombrich, E. (1995) *The Story of Art*, 16th edition. London: Phaidon Press. (First published 1950.)

Goode, T. (1988) Editorial, *Drama Broadsheet*, 5 (2), 1.

Goodman, N. (1976) *Languages of Art*. Indianapolis, IN: Hackett.

Gough, D. and Elbourne, D. (2002) 'Systematic Research Synthesis to Inform Policy, Practice and Democratic Debate', *Social Policy and Society* 1 (3), 225–236.

Graham, G. (2000) *Philosophy of the Arts*. London: Routledge. (First published 1997.)

Great Britain (1862) *Revised Code (Lowe)*. London: HMSO.

Great Britain (1870) *Education Act 1870*. London: HMSO.

Green, J., Camilli, G. and Elmore, P. (2006) *Handbook of Complementary Methods in Education Research*. Mahwah, NJ: Laurence Erlbaum.

Green, L. (2002) 'From the Western Classics to the World: Secondary Music Teachers' Changing Attitudes in England, 1982 and 1998', *Journal of Music Education*, 19 (1), 5–30.

Greene, M. (1995) *Releasing the Imagination: Essays on Education, the Arts, and Social Change*. San Francisco: Jossey-Bass.

Greer, G. (2011) 'Now Please Pay Attention Everybody. I'm About to Tell You What Art Is', *The Guardian*, 6 March.

Gribble, J. (1973) *Literary Education: A Re-Evaluation*. Cambridge: Cambridge University Press.

Guillory, J. (1993) *Cultural Capital: The Problem of Literary Canon Formation*. Chicago: University of Chicago Press.

Guthrie, J. (2004) 'Teaching for Literacy Engagement', *Journal of Literacy Research*, 36 (1), 1–29.

Guyer, P. (2004) 'The Origins of Modern Aesthetics: 1711–35', in Kivy, P. (ed.) *The Blackwell Guide to Aesthetics*. Oxford: Blackwell.

Habermas, J. (1987) *The Theory of Communicative Action*, Vol. 1. Cambridge: Polity Press.

Hagberg, G. (1995) *Art as Language: Wittgenstein, Meaning and Aesthetic Theory*. Ithaca, NY: Cornell University Press.

Hamilton, C. (2003) 'Art and Moral Education', in Bermúdez, J. and Gardner, S. (eds) *Art and Morality*. London: Routledge, 37–55.

Hammersley, M. (1997) 'Educational Research and Teaching: A Response to David Hargreaves' TTA Lecture', *British Educational Research Journal*, 23 (2), 141–161.

Hanfling, O. (ed.) (1992) *Philosophical Aesthetics: An Introduction*. Oxford: Blackwell.

Hargreaves, D. (1996) *Teaching as a Research-Based Profession*. TTA Annual Lecture. Online: eppi.ioe. ac.uk/cms/Portals/0/PDF%20reviews%20and%20summaries/TTA%20Hargreaves%20lecture.pdf

Harland, J. *et al.* (2000) *Arts Education in Secondary Schools: Effects and Effectiveness*. Slough: NFER.

Harris, J. (2001) *The New Art History: A Critical Introduction*. London: Routledge.

Hauser, A. (1962) *The Social History of Art*, Vol. 1. London: Routledge and Kegan Paul. (First published 1951.)

Haynes, A. (1987) 'The Dynamic Image: Changing Perspectives in Dance Education', in Abbs, P. (ed.) *Living Powers: The Arts in Education*. London: Falmer Press, 141–162.

Heathcote, D. and Bolton, G. (1994) *Drama For Learning: An Account of Heathcote's 'Mantle of the Expert'*. Portsmouth, NH: Heinemann.

Hegel, G. (2004) *Introductory Lectures on Aesthetics*. London: Penguin. (First published 1886.)

Herzog, P. (1996) 'The Condition to Which all Art Aspires: Reflections on Pater's Music', *British Journal of Aesthetics*, 36 (2), 122–134.

Hickman, R. (2005) *Why We Make Art and Why It Is Taught*. Bristol: Intellect Books.

Hirst, P. (1974) *Knowledge and the Curriculum: A Collection of Philosophical Papers*. London: Routledge and Kegan Paul.

Hobsbaum, P. (1972) *A Reader's Guide to Charles Dickens*. London: Thames & Hudson.

Holmes, E. (1911) *What Is and What Might Be*. London: Constable.

Hornbrook, D. (1989) *Education and Dramatic Art*. London: Blackwell Education.

Hornbrook, D. (1992) 'Confronting the Infant Phenomenon', *The English and Media Magazine*, Autumn, 18–21.

Hospers, J. (1969) 'The Concept of Artistic Expression', in Hospers, J. (ed.) *Introductory Readings in Aesthetics*. New York: Macmillan, 142–167. (First published 1955.)

Hughes, R. (1993) 'Tolstoy, Stanislavski, and the Art of Acting', *The Journal of Aesthetics and Art Criticism*, 51 (1), 39–48.

Hume, D. (2002) *Of the Standard of Taste* (first published 1757). Electronic resource with hyperlink annotations by Theodore Gracyk. Online: www.mnstate.edu/gracyk/courses/phil%20of%20art/hume%20on%20taste.htm

Inglis, F. (2004) *Culture*. Cambridge: Polity Press.

Isenberg, A. (1987) 'Analytical Philosophy and the Study of Art', *The Journal of Aesthetics and Art Criticism* (Special Issue: Analytic Aesthetics) 46, 125–136.

Iser, W. (1978) *The Act of Reading*. London: Routledge.

Iser, W. (1988) 'The Reading Process: A Phenomenological Approach', in Lodge, D. (ed.) *Modern Criticism and Theory*. London: Longman, 212–228.

Iser, W. (2001) *The Range of Interpretation*. New York: Columbia University Press.

Jaeger, R. (ed.) (1988) *Complementary Methods for Research in Education*. Washington, DC: American Educational Research Association.

Jakobson, R. (1988) 'Linguistics and Poetics', in Lodge, D. (ed.) *Modern Criticism and Theory*. London: Longman, 32–56.

Janik, A. (2001) *Wittgenstein's Vienna Revisited*. New Brunswick, NJ: Transaction Publishers.

Jenkins, K. (2003) *Re-Thinking History*, 3rd edition. London: Routledge. (First published 1991.)

Jewitt, C. (2008) *The Visual in Learning and Creativity*. London: Creative Partnerships, Arts Council England.

Johnson, P. (1989) 'Black Music, the Arts and Education', in Ross, M. (ed.) *The Claims of Feeling: Readings in Aesthetic Education*. London: Falmer Press.

Jones, J. (2008) 'Why This Is the Most Beautiful Modern Painting in the World', *The Guardian*, 19 January.

Jones, K. (2009) *Culture and Creative Learning*. London: Creative Partnerships, Arts Council England.

Kaestle, C. (1993) 'The Awful Reputation of Educational Research', *Research News and Comment*, January–February, 23–31.

Kant, I. (1928) *The Critique of Judgement* (trans. J. Meredith). Oxford: Clarendon Press. (First published 1790.)

Kaufman, J. and Baer, J. (eds) (2006) *Creativity and Reason in Cognitive Development*. Cambridge: Cambridge University Press.

Kaufman, J. and Sternberg, R. (eds) (2006) *The International Handbook of Creativity*. Cambridge: Cambridge University Press.

Kaufman, J. and Sternberg, R. (eds) (2010) *The Cambridge Handbook of Creativity*. Cambridge: Cambridge University Press.

Kelly, M. (ed.) (1998) *Encyclopedia of Aesthetics* (4 vols). Oxford: Oxford University Press.

Kieran, M. (2005) *Revealing Art*. London: Routledge.

Kivy, P. (ed.) (2004) *The Blackwell Guide to Aesthetics*. Oxford: Blackwell.

Klages, M. (2006) *Literary Theory: A Guide for the Perplexed*. London: Continuum.

Kok, K. (2011) *The Rationale for Visual Arts Education in Singapore: Analysis of Policies and Opinions*, Doctoral thesis, Durham University.

Koopman, C. (2005) 'Art as Fulfilment: On the Justification of Education in the Arts', *Journal of Philosophy of Education*, 39 (1), 85–97.

Korsmeyer, C. (2001) 'Taste', in Gaut, B. and Lopes, D. (eds) *The Routledge Companion to Aesthetics*. London: Routledge, 193–202.

Lamarque, P. and Olsen, S. (2004a) 'The Philosophy of Literature: Pleasure Restored', in Kivy, P. (ed.) *The Blackwell Guide to Aesthetics*. Oxford: Blackwell.

Lamarque, P. and Olsen, S. (eds) (2004b) *Aesthetics and the Philosophy of Art*. Oxford: Blackwell.

Langer, S. (1953) *Feeling and Form*. London: Routledge and Kegan Paul.

Law, J. (2004) *After Method: Mess in Social Science Research*. London: Routledge.

Leavy, P. (2009) *Method Meets Art: Arts-Based Research Practice*. New York: The Guilford Press.

Leuthhold, S. (2011) *Cross-Cultural Issues in Art*. London: Routledge.

Levinson, J. (1993) 'Extending Art Historically', *The Journal of Aesthetics and Art Criticism* 51 (3), 411–423.

Levinson, J. (2006) *Contemplating Art – Essays in Aesthetics*. Oxford: Oxford University Press. Oxford Scholarship Online: dx.doi.org/10.1093/acprof:oso/9780199206179.001.0001 (retrieved 15 July 2011).

Lewicki, T. (1996) *From 'Play Way' to 'Dramatic Art'*. Rome: Libreria Ateneo Salesiano.

Liamputtong, P. and Rumbold, J. (eds) (2008) *Knowing Differently: Arts-Based and Collaborative Research Methods*. New York: Nova Science Publishers.

Little, F. (2009) *An Exploration into the Uptake Rates of GCSE Music with a Focus on the Purposes of Music in School*. Doctoral thesis, Durham University.

Locke, J. (1968) 'Some Thoughts Concerning Education', in Axtell, J. (ed.) *The Educational Writings of John Locke*. Cambridge: Cambridge University Press, 114.

Lodge, D. (ed.) (1988) *Modern Criticism and Theory*. London: Longman.

Logan, R. (1986) 'A Conception of the Self in the Later Middle Ages', *Journal of Medieval History*, 12, 253–268.

Lord, C. (1994) 'Why Do We Take Serious Art Seriously?', *Journal of Aesthetic Education*, 28 (1), 40–46.

Lovlie, L. and Standish, P. (2002) 'Introduction: *Bildung* and the idea of a liberal education', *Journal of the Philosophy of Education*, 36 (3), 317–340.

Lyas, C. (1997) *Aesthetics*. London: University of London Press.

McBain, W. (1961) 'Noise, the "Arousal Hypothesis," and Monotonous Work', *Journal of Applied Psychology*, 45 (5), 309–317.

Macdonald, S. (1970) *The History and Philosophy of Art Education*. London: University of London Press.

McGilchrist, I. (2009) *The Master and His Emissary: The Divided Brain and the Making of the Western World*. New Haven, CT: Yale University Press.

McGregor, M., Tate, M. and Robinson, K. (eds) (1977) *Learning Through Drama*. London: Heinemann.

MacMurray, J. (1933) *Some Makers of the Modern Spirit*. London: Methuen.

McNiff, S. (1998) *Art-Based Research*. London: Jessica Kingsley.

Mandelbaum, M. (1965) 'Family Resemblances and Generalizations Concerning the Arts', *American Philosophical Quarterly*, 2, 219–228.

Margolis, J. (1985) 'Emergence and Creativity', in Mitias, M. (ed.) *Creativity in Art, Religion and Culture*. Amsterdam: Rodopi, 12–25.

Margolis, J. (2001) 'Medieval Aesthetics', in Gaut, B. and Lopes, D. (eds) *The Routledge Companion to Aesthetics*. London: Routledge, 27–36.

Marsh, J. (2010) *Childhood, Culture and Creativity*. London: Creative Partnerships, Arts Council England.

Martin, J. (1997) 'Inventing Sincerity, Refashioning Prudences: The Discovery of the Individual in Renaissance Europe', *The American Historical Review* 102 (5), 1309–1342.

Meeson, P. (1991) 'The Influence of Modernism on Art Education', *British Journal of Aesthetics*, 31 (2), 103–110.

Midgley, M. (1995) *Beast and Man: The Roots of Human Nature*, revised edition. London: Routledge. (First published 1979.)

Monk, R. (1991) *Ludwig Wittgenstein: The Duty of Genius*. London: Vintage Books.

Monk, R. (1999) 'Wittgenstein and the Two Cultures', *Prospect*, July, 66–67.

Morris, R. (1987) 'Towards a Shared Symbolic Order', in Abbs, P. (ed.) *Living Powers: The Arts in Education*. London: Falmer Press, 183–204.

Mortimer, A. (2000) 'Arts Education in the 21st Century – Frill or Fundamental?', *Education 3–13*, June, 2–8.

Mulhall, R. (1992) 'Expression', in Cooper, D. (ed.) *A Companion to Aesthetics*. Oxford: Blackwell.

Murphy, R. and Espeland, M. (2007) 'Making Connections in Assessment and Evaluation in Arts Education', in Bresler, L. (ed.) *International Handbook of Research in Arts Education Part 1*. Dordrecht: Springer, 337–340.

National Advisory Committee on Creative and Cultural Education (NACCCE) (1999) *All Our Futures*. Department for Education and Employment and Department for Culture, Media and Sport. London: DfEE.

National Curriculum Council (1990) *Drama and the National Curriculum*, Poster. London: HMSO.

Neelands, J. (1992) *Learning Through Imagined Experience*. London: Hodder & Stoughton.

Neelands, J. and Choe, B. (2010) 'The English Model of Creativity: Cultural Politics of an Idea', *International Journal of Cultural Policy*, 16 (3), 287–304.

Nochlin, L. (1971) 'Why Have There Been No Great Women Artists?', *ARTnews*, January, 22–39.

Nunn, P. (1920) *Education: Its Data and First Principles*. London: Edward Arnold.

Nusbaum, M. (1990) *Love's Knowledge: Essays on Philosophy and Literature*. Oxford: Oxford University Press.

Oakley, K. (2009) *'Art Works': Cultural Labour Markets*. London: Creative Partnerships, Arts Council England.

Oceana, A. and Pring, R. (2008) 'The Importance of Being Thorough: On Systematic Accumulations of "What Works" in Educational Research', *Journal of Philosophy of Education*, 42 (1), 15–39.

O'Connor, J. (2010) *Creative and Cultural Industries*. London: Creative Partnerships, Arts Council England.

OfSTED (1998) *The Arts Inspected*. London: Heinemann.

O'Neill, C. and Lambert, A. (1982) *Drama Structures: A Practical Handbook for Teachers*. London: Hutchinson.

Opie, C. (2004) *Doing Educational Research*. London: Sage.

Oreck, B. (2007) 'To See and to Share: Evaluating the Dance Experience in Education', in Bresler, L. (ed.) *International Handbook of Research in Arts Education, Part 1*. Dordrecht: Springer, 341–356.

Osborne, H. (1968) *Aesthetic and Art Theory: An Historical Introduction*. London: Longmans.

Osborne, H. (1984) 'Creativity, Progress and Personality', *Journal of Philosophy of Education*, 18 (2), 213–221.

O'Toole, J. (2009) 'Art, Creativity and Motivation', in Sinclair, C., Jeanneret, N. and O'Toole, J. (eds) *Education in the Arts*. Australia: Oxford University Press, 3–12.

Overgaard, S. (2007) *Wittgenstein and Other Minds*. London: Routledge.

Palmer, F. (1992) *Literature and Moral Understanding: A Philosophical Essay on Ethics, Aesthetics and Culture*. Oxford: Clarendon Press.

Pappas, N. (2001) 'Aristotle', in Gaut, B. and Lopes, D. (eds) *The Routledge Companion to Aesthetics*. London: Routledge, 15–26.

Parker, D. and Sefton-Green, J. (2010) Foreword to Fleming, M. *Arts in Education and Creativity*, 2nd edition. London: Arts Council.

Pater, W. (1986) *The Renaissance Studies in Art and Poetry* (ed. A. Philips). Oxford: Oxford University Press.

Patterson, A. (1992) 'Individualism in English: From Personal Growth to Discursive Construction', *English Education*, 24 (3), 131–146.

Peters, R. (ed.) (1969) *Perspectives on Plowden*. London: Routledge and Kegan Paul.

Pietschnig, J., Voracek, M. and Formann, A. (2010) 'Mozart Effect–Shmozart Effect: A Meta-Analysis', *Intelligence*, 38 (3), 314–323.

Pinker, S. (2002) *The Blank Slate*. London: Penguin.

Pitts, S. (2000) *A Century of Change in Music Education: Historical Perspectives on Contemporary Practice*. Aldershot: Ashgate.

Plato (1974) *The Republic*, 2nd edition. London: Penguin.

Plummeridge, C. (1991) *Music Education in Theory and Practice*. London: Falmer Press.

Plummeridge, C. (2001) 'The Justification for Music Education', in Philpott, C. and Plummeridge, C. (eds) *Issues in Music Teaching*. London: Routledge Falmer, 21–31.

Polity (1994) *The Polity Reader in Cultural Theory*. The Polity Press. Oxford: Blackwell.

Pollard, A. (1987) (ed.) *Children and Their Primary Schools: A New Perspective*. London: Falmer Press.

Pooke, G. and Newall, D. (2008) *Art History: The Basics*. London: Routledge.

Preen, D. (1999) 'Humpty Dumpty and the Nature of Poetic Understanding', *Use of English*, 50 (2), 112–114.

Pring, R. (2000) *Philosophy of Educational Research*. London: Continuum.

QCDA (2011) *The National Curriculum*. Online: www.qcda.gov.uk (retrieved April 2011).

Rauscher, F., Shaw, G. and Ky, C. (1993) 'Music and Spatial Task Performance', *Nature, International Weekly Journal of Science*, 365 (6447), 591–669.

Read, H. (1956) *Education Through Art*, 3rd edition. London: Faber & Faber. (First published 1943.)

Redfern, H. (1973) *Concepts in Modern Educational Dance*. London: Kimpton.

Reese, W. (2001) 'The Origins of Progressive Education', *History of Education Quarterly*, 41 (1), 1–24.

Reid, A. (1997) 'Value Pluralism and Physical Education', *European Physical Education Review*, 3 (1), 6–2.

Reid, L. (1969) *Meaning in the Arts*. London: George Allen & Unwin.

Richards, A. (2003) 'Arts and Academic Achievement in Reading: Functions and Implications', *Art Education*, 56 (6), 19–23.

Richardson, M. (1948) *Art and the Child*. London: University of London Press.

Richmond, S. (2009) 'Art Education as Aesthetic Education; A Response to Globalization', in Richmond, S. and Snowber, C. *Landscapes of Aesthetic Education*. Newcastle: Cambridge Scholars Publishing.

Richmond, S. (2010) 'Understanding Works of Art, the Inexpressible, and Teaching: A Philosophical Sketch', *International Journal of Education & the Arts*, 11 (Interlude 1). Online: www.ijea.org/v11i1/ (retrieved June 2011).

Ridley, A. (2007) *Nietzsche on Art*. London: Routledge.

Robinson, K. (1989) *The Arts in Schools: Principles, Practice and Provision*, 2nd edition. London: Calouste Gulbenkian Foundation.

Robinson, K. (2001) *Out of Our Minds: Learning to be Creative*, 2nd edition. Oxford: Capstone.

Rolling, J. (2008) 'Rethinking Relevance in Art Education: Paradigm Shifts and Policy Problematics in the Wake of the Information Age', *International Journal of Education and the Arts*, 9 (Interlude 1). Online: www.ijea.org/v9i1/ (retrieved June 2011).

Rollins, M. (2001) 'Pictorial Representation', in Gaut, B. and Lopes, D. (eds) *The Routledge Companion to Aesthetics*. London: Routledge, 297–312.

Rosenblatt, L. (1986) 'The Aesthetic Transaction', *Journal of Aesthetic Education*, 20 (4), 122–128.

Ross, M. (1978) *The Creative Arts*. London: Heinemann.

Ross, M. (1984) *The Aesthetic Impulse*. Oxford: Pergamon.

Ross, M. (ed.) (1989) *The Claims of Feeling: Readings in Aesthetic Education*. London: Falmer Press.

Rousseau, J. (1750) *Discourse on the Arts and Sciences*. Online: records.viu.ca/~johnstoi/rousseau/first discourse.htm (retrieved June 2011).

Rousseau, J. (1911) *Emile* (trans. B. Foxley). London: Dent. (First published 1762.) Online: www.gutenberg.org/ebooks/5427

Rowbottom, D. and Aiston, S. (2006) 'The Myth of "Scientific Method" in Contemporary Educational Research', *Journal of Philosophy of Education*, 40 (2), 137–156.

Sanderson, P. (1996) 'Dance Within the National Curriculum for Physical Education', *European Physical Education Review*, 2 (1), 54–63.

Sartwell, C. (1998) 'Art for Art's Sake', in Kelly, M. (ed.) *Encyclopedia of Aesthetics*. Oxford: Oxford University Press, 118–120.

Savile, A. (1982) *The Test of Time*. Oxford: Oxford University Press.

Schiller, F. (2004) *On the Aesthetic Education of Man*. New York: Dover Publications. (First published 1795.)

Schopenhauer, A. (1966) *The World as Will and Representation* (trans. E. Payne). New York: Dover Publications.

Schwartz, D. (1995) 'Can Intrinsic-Value Theorists Justify Subsidies for Contemporary Art?', *Public Affairs Quarterly*, 9 (4), 331–343.

Scruton, R. (2008) 'Photography and Representation', in Neill, A. and Ridley, A. (eds) *Arguing About Art*. London: Routledge, 213–232.

Secondary School Examinations Council (1943) *The Norwood Report: Report of the Committee of the Secondary School Examinations Council*. London: HMSO.

Sefton-Green, J. (ed.) (1999) *Creativity, Young People, and New Technologies: The Challenge of Digital Arts*. London: Routledge.

Sefton-Green, J. and Sinker, R. (eds) (2000) *Evaluating Creativity: Making and Learning by Young People*. London: Routledge.

Sefton-Green, J., Thompson, P., Jones, K. and Bresler, L. (eds) (2011) *The Routledge International Handbook of Creative Learning*. London: Routledge.

Sennett, R. (2008) *The Craftsman*. London: Penguin Books.

Shakespeare, W. (2008) *The Merchant of Venice*. Oxford: Oxford University Press.

Shiner, L. (2008) 'Western and Non-Western Concepts of Art', in Neill, A. and Ridley, A. (eds) *Arguing About Art*. London: Routledge, 464–470.

Shusterman, R. (2000a) *Performing Live: Aesthetic Alternatives for the Ends of Art*. Ithaca, NY: Cornell University Press.

Shusterman, R. (2000b) *Pragmatist Aesthetic: Living Beauty, Rethinking Art*, 2nd edition. New York: Rowman & Littlefield.

Shusterman, R. (2002) *Surface and Depth: Dialectics of Criticism and Culture*. Ithaca, NY: Cornell University Press.

Shusterman, R. (2003) 'Entertainment: A Question for Aesthetics', *British Journal of Aesthetics*, 43 (3), 289–307.

Shusterman, R. (2006) 'Thinking Through the Body, Educating for the Humanities: A Plea for Somaesthetics', *Journal of Aesthetic Education*, 40 (1), 1–21.

Shusterman, R. (2008) *Body Consciousness: A Philosophy of Mindfulness and Somaesthetics*. Cambridge: Cambridge University Press.

Sibley, F. (1959) 'Aesthetic Concepts', *Philosophical Review*, 68, 421–450. (Reprinted in Lamarque, P. and Olsen, S. (eds) (2004) *Aesthetics and the Philosophy of Art*. Oxford: Blackwell, 127–141.)

Sinclair, C., Jeanneret, N. and O'Toole, J. (eds) (2009) *Education in the Arts*. Australia: Oxford University Press.

Slade, P. (1954) *Child Drama*. London: University of London Press.

Smith, D. (2000) 'Introduction', in *Friedrich Nietzsche: The Birth of Tragedy*. Oxford: Oxford University Press.

Smith, R. (2008) 'Proteus Rising: Re-Imagining Educational Research', *Journal of Philosophy of Education*, 42 (S1), 183–198.

Smith, R. A. and Simpson, A. (eds) (1991) *Aesthetics and Arts Education*. Chicago: University of Illinois Press.

Spark, M. (1961) *The Prime of Miss Jean Brodie*. London: Penguin.

Spencer, H. (1929) *Education*. London: Watts and Company.

Spinks, J. (2011) *Letters From Wallsend*. Online: www.newpainters.com/. (See also: www.brooklyn publiclibrary.org/events/exhibitions/2011/wallsendbooklife.jsp)

Spivey, N. (2005) *How Art Made the World*. London: BBC Books.

Spruce, G. (2001) 'Music Assessment and Hegemony of Musical Heritage', in Philpott, C. and Plummeridge, C. (eds) *Issues in Music Teaching*. London: Routledge, 118–130.

Sternberg, R. and Lubart, T. (1999) 'The Concept of Creativity: Prospects and Paradigms', in Sternberg, R. J. (ed.) *Handbook of Creativity*. New York: Cambridge University Press, 3–15.

Stobart, G. (2008) *Testing Times: The Uses and Abuses of Assessment*. London: Routledge.

Stolnitz, J. (1969) 'The Aesthetic Attitude', in Hospers, J. (ed.) *Introductory Readings in Aesthetics*. New York: Macmillan.

Storey, J. (2001) *Culture Theory and Popular Culture*. London: Prentice Hall.

Sudano, G. and Sharpham, J. (1981) 'Back to Basics: Justifying the Arts in General Education', *Music Educators Journal*, 68 (3), 48–50.

Sutton, G. (1967) *Artisan or Artist? A History of the Teaching of Arts and Crafts in English Schools*. Oxford: Pergamon Press.

Swanwick, K. (1999) *Teaching Music Musically*. London: Routledge.

Taylor, P. (2000) *The Drama Classroom: Action, Reflection, Transformation*. London: RoutledgeFalmer.

Taylor, R. and Andrews, G. (1993) *The Arts in the Primary School*. London: Falmer Press.

Thomson, P. (2007) *Whole School Change*. London: Creative Partnerships, Arts Council England.

Tilghman, B. (1991) *Wittgenstein, Ethics and Aesthetics: The View from Eternity*. Albany: State University of New York Press.

Tolstoy, L. (1995) *What Is Art?* London: Duckworth. (First published 1898.)

Tooley, J. and Darby, D. (1998) *Educational Research – A Critique*. London: Office for Standards in Education.

Townley, B. and Beech, N. (2010) *Managing Creativity? Exploring the Paradox*. Cambridge: Cambridge University Press.

Turner, M. (ed.) (2006) *The Artful Mind: Cognitive Science and the Riddle of Human Creativity*. Oxford: Oxford University Press.

Van den Berg, J. (1961) *The Changing Nature of Man*. New York: Norton.

Varkoy, O. (2010) 'The Concept of *Bildung*', *Philosophy of Music Education Review*, 18 (1), 85–96.

Vygotsky, L. (1962) *Thought and Language*, Cambridge, MA: MIT Press.

Warburton, N. (2003) *The Art Question*. London: Routledge.

Ward, S. (2010) *Understanding Creative Partnerships: An Examination of Policy and Practice*. PhD thesis, Durham University.

Ward, S. and Bagley, C. (2010) 'Review of Method Meets Art: Arts-Based Research Practice', *Qualitative Research*, 10 (2), 273–277.

Way, B. (1967) *Development Through Drama*. London: Longman.

Webster, P. (2007) 'Prelude: Knowledge, Skills, Attitudes, and Values: Technology and Its Role in Arts Education', in Bresler, L. (ed.) *International Handbook of Research in Arts Education*, Part 2. Dordrecht: Springer, 1293–1296.

Weitz, M. (1956) 'The Role of Theory in Aesthetics', *Journal of Aesthetics and Art Criticism*, 15, 27–35. (Reprinted in Lamarque, P. and Olsen, S. (eds) (2004) *Aesthetics and the Philosophy of Art*. Oxford: Blackwell, 12–18.)

White, J. (1995) 'Creativity', in Cooper, D. (ed.) *A Companion to Aesthetics*. Oxford: Blackwell. (First published 1992.)

Wicks, R. (2007) *Routledge Philosophy Guidebook to Kant on Judgement*. London: Routledge.

Wilkinson, A. (1987) 'Aspects of Communication and the Plowden Report', *Oxford Review of Education*, 13 (1), 111–118.

Wilkinson, R. (1992) 'Art, Emotion and Expression', in Hanfling, O. (ed.) *Philosophical Aesthetics: An Introduction*. Oxford: Blackwell, 179–238.

Williams, K. (2002) 'The Limits of Aesthetic Separatism: Literary Education and Michael Oakeshott's Philosophy of Art', *International Journal of Research and Method in Education*, 25 (2), 163–173.

Williams, R. (1961) *The Long Revolution*. Swansea: Parthian Books.

Willis, P. (1990) *Common Culture*. Milton Keynes: Open University Press.

Winner, E. and Hetland, L. (2000) 'The Arts in Education: Evaluating the Evidence for a Causal Link', *Journal of Aesthetic Education*, 34 (3), 3–10.

Winston, J. (2010) *Beauty and Education*. London: Routledge.

Witkin. R. (1974) *The Intelligence of Feeling*. London: Heinemann.

Wittgenstein, L. (1953, 2nd edn 1958) *Philosophical Investigations* (trans. G. E. M. Anscombe). Oxford: Basil Blackwell.

Wittgenstein, L. (1961) *Tractatus Logico Philosophicus* (trans. C. Ogden and F. Ramsey). London: Routledge and Kegan Paul. (First published 1922.)

Wittgenstein, L. (1969a) *On Certainty*. Oxford: Blackwell.

Wittgenstein, L. (1969b) *The Blue and Brown Books*. Oxford: Basil Blackwell.

Wittgenstein, L. (1998) *Culture and Value*, revised 2nd edition. Oxford: Blackwell.

Young, J. (2010) 'Art and the Educated Audience', *The Journal of Aesthetic Education*, 44 (3), 29–42.

Index